Lecture Notes in Control and Information Sciences

Edited by A.V. Balakrishnan and M.Thoma

20

Bo Egardt

Stability of Adaptive Controllers

Springer-Verlag
Berlin Heidelberg New York 1979

Author
Dr. Bo Egardt
Dept. of Automatic Control
Lund Institute of Technology
S-220 07 Lund 7

ISBN 3-540-09646-9 Springer-Verlag Berlin Heidelberg New York
ISBN 0-387-09646-9 Springer-Verlag New York Heidelberg Berlin

Printed in Germany

Printing and binding: Beltz Offsetdruck, Hemsbach/Bergstr.
2060/3020-543210

Preface

The present work is concerned with the stability analysis of adaptive control systems in both discrete and continuous time. The attention is focussed on two well-known approaches, namely the model reference adaptive systems and the self-tuning regulators. The two approaches are treated in a general framework, which leads to the formulation of a fairly general algorithm. The stability properties of this algorithm are analysed and sufficient conditions for boundedness of closed-loop signals are given. The analysis differs from most other studies in this field in that disturbances are introduced in the problem.

Most of the material was originally presented as a Ph.D. thesis at the Department of Automatic Control, Lund Institute of Technology, Lund, Sweden, in December 1978. It is a pleasure for me to thank my supervisor, Professor Karl Johan Åström, who proposed the problem and provided valuable guidance throughout the work.

B. Egardt

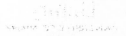

Table of contents

1. INTRODUCTION 1

2. UNIFIED DESCRIPTION OF DISCRETE TIME CONTROLLERS 9

   2.1 Design method for known plants 9
   2.2 Class of adaptive controllers 13
   2.3 Example of the general control scheme 20
   2.4 The positive real condition 24

3. UNIFIED DESCRIPTION OF CONTINUOUS TIME CONTROLLERS 27

   3.1 Design method for known plants 27
   3.2 Class of adaptive controllers 30
   3.3 Examples of the general control scheme 35
   3.4 The positive real condition 41

4. STABILITY OF DISCRETE TIME CONTROLLERS 43

   4.1 Preliminaries 45
   4.2 L^{∞}-stability 60
   4.3 Convergence in the disturbance-free case 77
   4.4 Results on other configurations 80
   4.5 Discussion 84

5. STABILITY OF CONTINUOUS TIME CONTROLLERS 87

   5.1 Preliminaries 87
   5.2 L^{∞}-stability 95
   5.3 Convergence in the disturbance-free case 103

REFERENCES 107

APPENDIX A - PROOF OF THEOREM 4.1 111

APPENDIX B - PROOF OF THEOREM 5.1 132

1. INTRODUCTION

Generalities

Most of the current techniques to design control systems are based on knowledge of the plant and its environment. In many cases this information is, however, not available. The reason might be that the plant is too complex or that basic relationships are not fully understood, or that the process and the disturbances may change with operating conditions. Different possibilities to overcome this difficulty exist.

One way to attack the problem is to apply some system identification technique to obtain a model of the process and its environment from practical experiments. The controller design is then based on the resulting model. Another possibility is to adjust the parameters of the controller during plant operation. This can be done manually as is normally done for ordinary PID-controllers, provided that only a few parameters have to be adjusted. Manual adjustment is, however, not feasible if more than three parameters have to be adjusted. Some kind of automatic adjustment of the controller parameters is then needed.

Adaptive control is one possibility to tune the controller. In particular, *self-tuning regulators* and *model reference adaptive systems* are two widely discussed approaches to solve the problem for plants with unknown parameters. These techniques will be the main concern of the present work. Although these two approaches in practice can handle slowly time-varying plants, the design is basically made for constant but unknown plants. The basic ideas behind the two techniques are discussed below.

Self-tuning regulators

The self-tuning regulators (STR) are based on a fairly natural combination of identification and control. A design method for known plants is the starting-point. Since the plant is unknown, the parameters of the controller can, however, not be determined. They are instead obtained from a recursive parameter estimator. A separation between identification and control is thus assumed. Note that the only information from the estimator that is used by the control law is the parameter estimates. Schemes which utilize e.g. parameter uncertainties are not considered here.

Probably the first to formulate this simple idea as an algorithm was Kalman (1958). An on-line least-squares algorithm produced estimates of plant parameters. The estimates were then used at every sampling instant to compute a deadbeat control law.

The self-tuning idea was brought up by Peterka (1970) and Åström/Wittenmark (1973) in a stochastic framework. Åström and Wittenmark's algorithm, based on minimum variance control, is described below in a simple case.

EXAMPLE 1.1

Consider the plant, given by

$$y(t) + ay(t-1) = bu(t-1) + e(t),$$

where u is the input, y the output and $\{e(t)\}$ is a sequence of independent, zero-mean random variables. It is easy to see that the control law

$$u(t) = \frac{a}{b}\, y(t)$$

gives the minimum output variance. If the parameters a and b are unknown, the algorithm by Åström and Wittenmark can be applied. It consists of two steps, each repeated at every sampling instant:

1. Estimate the parameter α in the model

   $$y(t) = \alpha y(t-1) + \beta_0 u(t-1) + \varepsilon(t),$$

   e.g. by minimizing $\sum^{t} \varepsilon^2(s)$. Denote the resulting estimate by $\hat{\alpha}(t)$.

2. Use the control law

$$u(t) = - \frac{\hat{\alpha}(t)}{\beta_0} y(t).$$

It should be noted that the estimation of α can be made recursively if a least-squares criterion is used. This makes the scheme practically feasible. □

The above algorithm can easily be generalized to higher order plants with time delays. The paper by Åström and Wittenmark (1973) presented some analysis of the algorithm. The main conclusion was that *if* the algorithm converges at all, then it converges to the desired minimum variance controller, even if the noise $\{e(t)\}$ is correlated. The latter result was somewhat surprising at that point. It has later been shown by Ljung (1977a) that the algorithm converges under a stability condition if the noise characteristics satisfy a certain positive realness condition. Similar results without the stability assumption was given by Goodwin et al. (1978b).

The self-tuning regulators are not confined to minimum variance control. For example, Åström/Wittenmark (1974) and Clarke/Gawthrop (1975) proposed generalizations of the basic algorithm. Algorithms based on pole placement design were discussed by Edmunds (1976), Wellstead et al. (1978) and Åström et al. (1978). Multivariable formulations are given by e.g. Borisson (1978).

The general configuration of a self-tuning regulator is shown in Fig. 1.1. The regulator can be thought of as composed of three parts: a parameter estimator, a controller, and a third part, which relates the controller parameters to the parameter estimates. This partitioning of the regulator is convenient when describing how it works and to derive algorithms. The regulator could, however, equally well be described as a single nonlinear regulator. There are of course many design methods and identification techniques that can be combined into a self-tuning regulator with this general structure. A survey of the field is given in Åström et al. (1977).

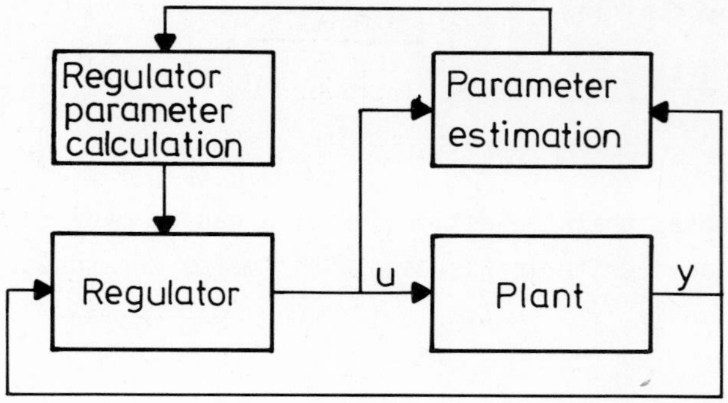

Figure 1.1. Block diagram of a self-tuning regulator.

Model reference adaptive systems

The area of model reference adaptive systems (MRAS) is more difficult to characterize in a general way. The main reason is that the many different schemes proposed have been motivated by different considerations.

An early attempt to cope with e.g. gain variations in servo problems was Whitaker's "MIT-rule". Parks (1966) initiated a rapid development of the MRAS by using Lyapunov functions and stability theory in the design. He also observed the relevance of a certain positive realness condition. A simple example will illustrate the ideas.

EXAMPLE 1.2

A first order plant is assumed to have known time constant but unknown gain. The desired relationship between the input u and the output y is defined by a reference model with output y^M, see Fig. 1.2. The objective is thus to adjust the gain K such that $e(t) = y(t) - y^M(t)$ tends to zero. The solution uses a Lyapunov function

$$V = \frac{1}{2}\,(e^2 + c\tilde{K}^2),$$

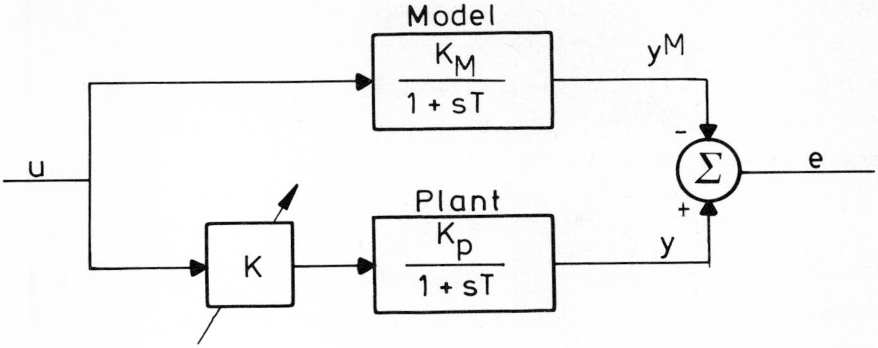

Figure 1.2. Configuration of Example 1.2.

where $c > 0$ and

$$\tilde{K} = K_M - KK_p.$$

The derivative of V is

$$\dot{V} = -\frac{1}{T}e^2 + \frac{1}{T}\tilde{K}ue + c\tilde{K}\dot{\tilde{K}}.$$

If the gain is adjusted according to

$$\dot{\tilde{K}} = -\frac{1}{cT}ue, \tag{1.1}$$

the derivative of V is negative definite and it can be shown that the error e tends to zero. This implies that the objective is fulfilled. Note that (1.1) can equivalently be written as

$$\dot{K} = \frac{1}{cTK_p}ue$$

if K_p is assumed to be constant. Since c is arbitrary, this updating formula is possible to implement, although the adaptation rate will vary due to the unknown plant gain. □

The above example can be generalized considerably. The problem to follow a given reference signal was solved for higher order plants with unknown dynamics, see e.g. Gilbart et al. (1970) and Monopoli (1973). However, a crucial assumption in these references is that the plant's transfer function has a pole excess (i.e. difference between number of poles and number of zeros) equal to one. Monopoli (1974) proposed a modification of the earlier schemes to treat the general case. His ideas have inspired many authors in the field and in particular the stability problem associated with his scheme has been frequently discussed.

The basic idea behind the schemes can be described as in Fig. 1.3. The unknown plant is controlled by an adjustable controller. The desired behaviour of the plant is defined by a reference model. Some kind of adaptation mechanism modifies the parameters of the adjustable controller to minimize the difference between the plant output and the desired output. The methods to design the adaptation loop in MRAS have mostly been based on stability theory since Park's important paper appeared. Although the MRAS ideas were first developed for continuous time control, the same framework has been carried over to discrete time control. Surveys of the numerous variants of the technique are given by e.g. Landau (1974) and Narendra/Valavani (1976).

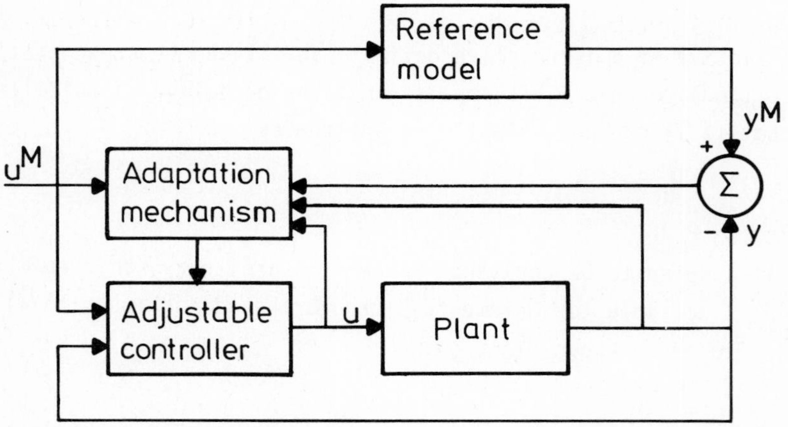

Figure 1.3. Block diagram of a model reference adaptive regulator.

Similarities between STR and MRAS

The STR and the MRAS were developed to solve different problems. The STR were originally designed to solve the stochastic regulator problem. The MRAS were developed to solve the deterministic servo problem. In spite of these differences, the two techniques exhibit some important similarities. This has been observed in e.g. Ljung (1977a) and Gawthrop (1977). The question has thus arised, whether the two approaches are more closely related than earlier thought. Some answers are given in Ljung/Landau (1978), Narendra/Valavani (1978) and Egardt (1978).

The purpose of the first part of this work is to describe several MRAS and STR in a unified manner. The discussion is limited to systems with one input and one output. It is assumed that only the plant output is available for feedback. It will be shown that it is possible to derive MRAS from the STR point of view. This observation leads to the possibility to describe several MRAS and STR as special cases of a fairly general algorithm. The unified treatment also facilitates a comparison of the positive real conditions, which play an important role in the design and analysis of both MRAS and STR. It is shown that the condition can be removed in the deterministic case.

The discrete time case is covered by Chapter 2 and Chapter 3 gives the treatment for continuous time control. Since adaptive regulators are predominantly implemented using digital computers, the discrete time case is emphasized. The analysis is also a little simpler in that case.

Stability

There are a number of important properties of adaptive regulators which are poorly understood, e.g.

- overall stability
- convergence of the regulator
- properties of the possible limiting regulators
- effects of disturbances.

Overall stability of the closed loop system is perhaps the most fundamental property. This is of course important both practically and theoretically. The stability problem has also been encountered indirectly in most convergence studies. For MRAS without disturbances, boundedness of closed-loop signals was assumed to prove convergence of the output error to zero. See e.g. Feuer/Morse (1977), Narendra/Valavani (1978) and - for discrete time - Landau/Bêthoux (1975). The paper by Feuer and Morse (1977) in fact contained a proof of global stability, but the algorithm considered was very complicated. For simpler schemes, the only rigorous convergence proofs without the stability requirement are the ones by Goodwin et al. (1978a) for discrete time, Egardt (1978) for both discrete and continuous time and Morse (1979) for continuous time. Goodwin et al. and Morse treat the disturbance-free case whereas Egardt (1978) contains results with disturbances, too.

Stability conditions are important also in the stochastic convergence analysis of STR. The convergence results presented in Ljung (1977a) for the minimum variance self-tuning regulator required a stability assumption. As mentioned above, similar results were given by Goodwin et al. (1978b) without the stability condition.

Stability analysis of adaptive schemes in the presence of disturbances is the topic of the second part. The stability properties of the algorithms described in Chapters 2 and 3 are investigated using the L^∞-stability concept. The main effort is given to algorithms with a stochastic approximation type of estimation scheme. The main results (Theorems 4.1 and 5.1) state that the closed-loop signals remain bounded under some reasonable assumptions. The most important one - boundedness of parameter estimates - can be omitted if the algorithms are slightly modified. When no disturbances affect the plant, the stability results can be used to prove convergence of the output error to zero. This result thus holds without a priori requiring the closed loop to be stable and is analogous to the above mentioned results by Goodwin et al. (1978a) and Morse (1979). Chapter 4 treats the discrete time case and the continuous time schemes are analysed in Chapter 5.

2. UNIFIED DESCRIPTION OF DISCRETE TIME CONTROLLERS

The MRAS philosophy has been applied to the discrete time case in e.g. Landau/Běthoux (1975), Běnějean (1977), and Ionescu/Monopoli (1977). Stability theory is the major design tool. The STR approach has been used almost exclusively for discrete time systems, see e.g. Åström/Wittenmark (1973), Clarke/Gawthrop (1975), and Åström et al. (1978). The basic idea is to use a certainty equivalence structure, i.e. to use a control law for the known parameter case and just replace the unknown parameters by their estimates.

Since the control algorithms obtained by the MRAS and the STR approaches are very similar, it is of interest to investigate the connections between the two approaches. Results in this direction are given in Gawthrop (1977) and Ljung/Landau (1978). A unified treatment of MRAS and STR for problems with output feedback will be presented in this chapter. It will be shown that MRAS can be derived from the STR point of view. Some problems in the design and analysis of the discrete time schemes are also discussed. In particular, the nature of the positive real condition, associated with both MRAS and STR, will be examined in detail. It is shown that this condition can be avoided in the deterministic case.

2.1. Design method for known plants

A design method, which will be the basis for the general adaptive algorithm in the next section, is described below. It consists of a pole placement combined with zero cancellation and adding of new zeros. Related schemes are given in e.g. Běnějean (1977), Ionescu/Monopoli (1977), Gawthrop (1977), and Åström et al. (1978).

The plant is assumed to satisfy the difference equation

$$A(q^{-1})\ y(t) = q^{-(k+1)}\ b_0\ B(q^{-1})\ u(t) + w(t), \tag{2.1}$$

where q^{-1} is the backward shift operator, k is a nonnegative integer, and $A(q^{-1})$ and $B(q^{-1})$ are polynomials defined by

$$A(q^{-1}) = 1 + a_1 q^{-1} + \ldots + a_n q^{-n}$$

$$B(q^{-1}) = 1 + b_1 q^{-1} + \ldots + b_m q^{-m}.$$

Furthermore, $w(t)$ is a nonmeasurable disturbance.

REMARK

The parameter b_0 is not included in the B-polynomial, because it will be treated in a special way in the estimation part of the adaptive controller in the next section. □

The objective of the controller design is to make the difference between the plant output $y(t)$ and the reference model output $y^M(t)$ as small as possible. The reference output y^M is related to the command input u^M by the reference model, given by

$$y^M(t) = \frac{q^{-(k+1)}\, B^M(q^{-1})}{A^M(q^{-1})}\, u^M(t) = \frac{q^{-(k+1)}(b_0^M + \ldots + b_m^M\, q^{-m})}{1 + a_1^M\, q^{-1} + \ldots + a_n^M\, q^{-n}}\, u^M(t). \tag{2.2}$$

It is no restriction to assume that the polynomial degrees n and m are the same in the model and the plant, because coefficients may be zero in (2.2) and it is easy to add zeros or poles by modifying u^M. It is seen that the time delay of the reference model is greater than or equal to the time delay of the plant. This is a natural assumption to avoid noncausal control laws.

The problem will be approached by assuming the controller configuration shown in Fig. 2.1. Here R, S, and T are polynomials in the backward shift operator. Motivation for this structure can be found in e.g. Åström et al. (1978). It can be shown that the controller is closely related to the solution in a state space setup with Kalman filter and feedback from the state estimates. Notice that the process zeros are cancelled. This implies that only minimum phase systems can be considered. Other versions which allow nonminimum phase systems are discussed in Åström et al. (1978). The T-polynomial can be interpreted as the characteristic polynomial of an observer.

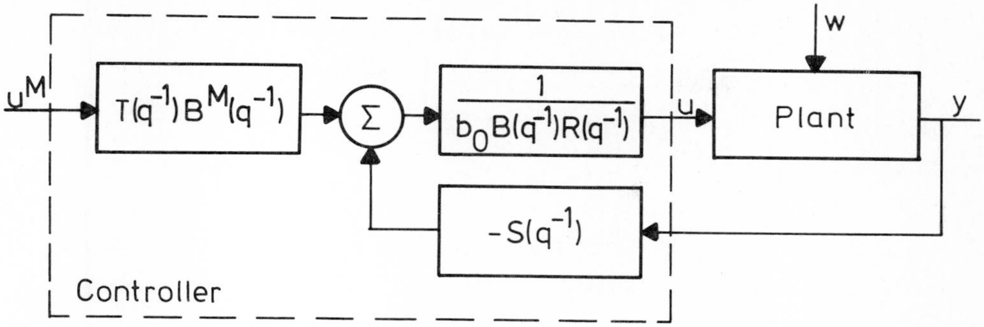

Figure 2.1. Controller configuration.

The design procedure will be given for two different problems. In the first one, the disturbances are neglected and the problem is treated as a pure servo-problem. This means that the design concentrates on tracking a given reference signal. The procedure will be referred to as a *deterministic* design. On the other hand, if the disturbance is considered as part of the problem, the controller should have a regulating property too. An interesting special case is when the disturbance w(t) is a moving average, given by

$$w(t) = C(q^{-1})\ v(t) = (1 + c_1 q^{-1} + \ldots + c_n q^{-n})\ v(t), \qquad (2.3)$$

where {v(t)} are independent, zero-mean random variables. A design procedure which has the objective to reject noise of the form (2.3), will be called *stochastic*. The deterministic design is considered first.

Deterministic design

Assuming w(t) = 0, it is possible to have the plant output equal to the reference model output $y^M(t)$. This is obtained by making the closed-loop transfer function equal to the reference model transfer function, i.e.

$$\frac{q^{-(k+1)}\,B^M(q^{-1})}{A^M(q^{-1})} = \frac{q^{-(k+1)}\,b_0\,B(q^{-1})T(q^{-1})B^M(q^{-1})}{A(q^{-1})\,b_0\,B(q^{-1})R(q^{-1}) + q^{-(k+1)}\,b_0\,B(q^{-1})S(q^{-1})}$$

or, equivalently,

$$T(q^{-1})\,A^M(q^{-1}) = A(q^{-1})\,R(q^{-1}) + q^{-(k+1)}\,S(q^{-1}). \tag{2.4}$$

The observer polynomial T is cancelled in the closed-loop transfer function. Neglecting the effects of initial values, it can therefore be chosen arbitrarily. When T has been determined, the equation (2.4) has many solutions R and S. It will, however, be required that the degree of R is less than or equal to the time delay k. Then there is a unique solution to (2.4). The degree of S will depend on n, k, and the degree of T. Furthermore, it is required that $R(0) \neq 0$ in order to get a causal control law. As seen from (2.4), this is equivalent to $T(0) \neq 0$. Finally the R- and T-polynomials are scaled so that $T(0) = R(0) = 1$.

The deterministic design procedure can thus be summarized in the following steps:

1) Choose the polynomial $T(q^{-1})$ defined by

$$T(q^{-1}) = 1 + t_1 q^{-1} + \ldots + t_{n_T}\, q^{-n_T}.$$

2) Solve the polynomial equation

$$T(q^{-1})\,A^M(q^{-1}) = A(q^{-1})\,R(q^{-1}) + q^{-(k+1)}\,S(q^{-1})$$

for the unique solutions $R(q^{-1})$ and $S(q^{-1})$, defined by

$$R(q^{-1}) = 1 + r_1 q^{-1} + \ldots + r_k q^{-k}$$

$$S(q^{-1}) = s_0 + s_1 q^{-1} + \ldots + s_{n_S}\, q^{-n_S}, \quad n_S = \max(n+n_T-k-1,\ n-1).$$

Stochastic design

The deterministic design procedure can of course be used also when disturbances are acting on the plant. The choice of observer polynomial will, however, be of importance not only during an initial transient period. If it is assumed that w(t) is given by (2.3), then it is well-known that the optimal choice of observer polynomial is

$$T(q^{-1}) = C(q^{-1}),$$

in the sense of minimum variance. This is explicitly demonstrated in Gawthrop (1977) as a generalization of the result on minimum variance regulators in Åström (1970).

2.2. Class of adaptive controllers

A general adaptive control scheme is defined in this section. The scheme is a self-tuning version of the controller described in the preceeding section. It will be shown to include earlier proposed MRAS and STR as special cases.

The plant is still assumed to satisfy (2.1). The following assumptions are also introduced.

A1) The number of plant poles n and zeros m are known.

A2) The time delay k is known and the sign of b_0 is known. Without loss of generality b_0 is assumed positive.

A3) The plant is minimum phase, i.e. the numerator polynomial $B(q^{-1})$ in (2.1) has its zeros outside the unit circle.

REMARK

Notice that some coefficients in $A(q^{-1})$ or $B(q^{-1})$ may be zero. It therefore suffices to know an upper bound on the polynomial degrees to put the equation into the form of (2.1) with known n and m. The condition on k in A2) is the counterpart of the continuous time condition, that the pole excess (i.e. the difference between the number of poles and number of zeros) is known. Compare Chapter 3. The minimum phase assumption was commented upon in Section 2.1. □

The objective of the controller is the same as in Section 2.1, i.e. to minimize the error defined by

$$e(t) = y(t) - y^M(t).$$

The controller to be described uses an *implicit* identification, Åström et al. (1978). This means that the controller parameters are estimated instead of the parameters of the model (2.1). The first step in the development of the algorithm is therefore to obtain a model of the plant, expressed in the unknown controller parameters. Thus, use the identity (2.4) and the equations (2.1) and (2.2) to write for the error:

$$TA^M e(t) = TA^M y(t) - TA^M y^M(t) = (AR + q^{-(k+1)}S)\, y(t) - TA^M y^M(t) =$$

$$= q^{-(k+1)}[b_0 BR\, u(t) + S\, y(t) - TB^M u^M(t)] + R\, w(t). \qquad (2.5)$$

To obtain some flexibility of the model structure, a filtered version of the error will be considered. Let Q and P be asymptotically stable polynomials, defined by

$$Q(q^{-1}) = 1 + q_1 q^{-1} + \ldots + q_{n_Q} q^{-n_Q}$$

$$P(q^{-1}) = P_1(q^{-1})\, P_2(q^{-1}) = 1 + p_1 q^{-1} + \ldots + p_{n_P} q^{-n_P},$$

where P_1 and P_2 are factors of P of degree n_{P_1} and n_{P_2} respectively. It is assumed that $P_1(0) = P_2(0) = 1$. Define the filtered error by

$$e_f(t) = \frac{Q(q^{-1})}{P(q^{-1})}\, e(t).$$

Note that $e_f(t)$ is a known quantity, because y(t) is measured and $y^M(t)$, Q, and P are known. Using (2.5), $e_f(t)$ can be written as

$$e_f(t) = \frac{Q}{TA^M}\, q^{-(k+1)} \left[\frac{b_0 BR}{P}\, u(t) + \frac{S}{P}\, y(t) - \frac{TB^M}{P}\, u^M(t)\right] + \frac{QR}{TA^M P}\, w(t) =$$

$$= \frac{Q}{TA^M}\, q^{-(k+1)} \left[b_0 \frac{u(t)}{P_1} + b_0 (BR - P_2) \frac{u(t)}{P} + S \frac{y(t)}{P} - \frac{TB^M}{P}\, u^M(t)\right] + \frac{QR}{TA^M P}\, w(t). \qquad (2.6)$$

REMARK

The polynomials Q and P give the necessary flexibility to cover both MRAS and STR. The exact choices of the polynomials and their degrees will be commented in the examples in Section 2.3. It should also be noted that instead of polynomials Q and P, one could consider rational functions. We will however not elaborate this case. □

The general adaptive controller will first be given for the deterministic design case.

Deterministic design

The observer polynomial is now determined a priori. Let θ be a vector, containing the unknown parameters of the polynomials $BR-P_2$ and S/b_0 and the constant $1/b_0$ as the last element. Note that θ contains the parameters of the controller, described in Section 2.1.

Furthermore, define the vector $\varphi(t)$ from

$$\varphi^T(t) = \left[\frac{u(t-1)}{P}, \frac{u(t-2)}{P}, \ldots, \frac{y(t)}{P}, \frac{y(t-1)}{P}, \ldots, -\frac{TB^M}{P} u^M(t)\right], \quad (2.7)$$

where the numbers of u- and y-terms are compatible with the definition of θ. Note that the elements of φ are known signals.

Using the definitions of θ and φ, it is possible to write (2.6) as

$$e_f(t) = \frac{Q}{TA^M} q^{-(k+1)} \left[b_0 \frac{u(t)}{P_1} + b_0 \theta^T \varphi(t)\right] + \frac{QR}{TA^M P} w(t). \quad (2.8)$$

This model, which contains the unknown controller parameters b_0 and θ, can be taken as a basis for a class of adaptive controllers. The intention is to estimate the unknown parameters b_0 and θ, and to use these estimates in the control law. The estimation procedure can be designed e.g. to force a prediction error of $e_f(t)$ to zero. Note that $e_f(t)$ is itself a known quantity. Taking the different possibilities of choosing e.g. estimation algorithm and control law into consideration, a class of controllers can be characterized in the following way.

BASIC CONTROL SCHEME

- o Estimate the unknown parameters b_0 and θ (or some combination of these) in the model (2.8).
- o Use these estimates to determine the control signal.

A natural requirement on the controller is that it performs as the controller in Section 2.1, if the parameter estimates are equal to the true parameters.

Stochastic design

The algorithm described above can of course be used also when $w \neq 0$. However, if w(t) is given by (2.3) with an unknown C-polynomial, it was seen in Section 2.1 that the choice T = C is optimal. Since C is unknown, it might be desirable to estimate it. Some minor changes are then needed. Concatenate the θ-vector with a vector whose elements are the unknown parameters of C/b_0. Also, redefine the φ-vector as

$$\varphi^T(t) = \left[\frac{u(t-1)}{P}, \frac{u(t-2)}{P}, \ldots, \frac{y(t)}{P}, \frac{y(t-1)}{P}, \ldots, -\frac{B^M}{P} u^M(t), -\frac{B^M}{P} u^M(t-1), \ldots\right] \tag{2.9}$$

The filtered error can then be written as

$$e_f(t) = \frac{Q}{CA^M} q^{-(k+1)}\left[b_0 \frac{u(t)}{P_1} + b_0 \theta^T \varphi(t)\right] + \frac{QR}{A^M P} v(t), \tag{2.10}$$

which constitutes the model for a class of algorithms in the same way as in the deterministic design case.

The class of algorithms described above contains many different schemes. Apart from the selection of the polynomials Q and P and the choice between fixed or estimated observer polynomial, the choices of control law and estimation algorithm generate different schemes. The choice of estimation algorithm will be commented in connection with some examples in Section 2.3 and further discussed in Section 2.4. To proceed, it is however suitable to specify one particular method.

A special parameter estimator

A characteristic feature of the model reference methods is that the estimation is based on a model like (2.8), where the parameters b_0 and θ enter *bilinearly*. The estimation scheme will be described in the deterministic design case.

Let $\hat{b}_0(t-1)$ and $\hat{\theta}(t-1)$ denote estimates at time t-1 of b_0 and θ. Using the model (2.8), a one step ahead prediction of $e_f(t)$ is defined as

$$\hat{e}_f(t|t-1) = \frac{Q}{TA^M}\left[\hat{b}_0(t-1)\,\frac{u(t-k-1)}{P_1} + \hat{b}_0(t-1)\,\hat{\theta}^T(t-1)\,\varphi(t-k-1)\right]. \tag{2.11}$$

The prediction error $\varepsilon(t)$ is defined as

$$\varepsilon(t) = e_f(t) - \hat{e}_f(t|t-1), \tag{2.12}$$

where $e_f(t)$ is given by (2.8), and is usually used in the parameter updating. The following expression is obtained for $\varepsilon(t)$ if it is assumed that the disturbance w(t) is equal to zero:

$$\varepsilon(t) = \frac{Q}{TA^M}\Big[[b_0 - \hat{b}_0(t-1)]\left(\frac{u(t-k-1)}{P_1} + \hat{\theta}^T(t-1)\,\varphi(t-k-1)\right) + \\ + b_0[\theta - \hat{\theta}(t-1)]^T\,\varphi(t-k-1)\Big]. \tag{2.13}$$

The following parameter updating is used in the constant gain case:

$$\begin{pmatrix} \hat{b}_0(t) \\ \hat{\theta}(t) \end{pmatrix} = \begin{pmatrix} \hat{b}_0(t-1) \\ \hat{\theta}(t-1) \end{pmatrix} + \Gamma \begin{pmatrix} \frac{u(t-k-1)}{P_1} + \hat{\theta}^T(t-1)\,\varphi(t-k-1) \\ \varphi(t-k-1) \end{pmatrix} \varepsilon(t), \tag{2.14}$$

where Γ is a constant, positive definite matrix.

REMARK

It is straightforward to define stochastic approximation (SA) or least squares (LS) versions of the algorithm (2.14). For LS Γ is replaced by $P(t) = [\sum^t \psi(s)\,\psi(s)^T]^{-1}$ and a SA variant uses e.g. $1\,/\,\mathrm{tr}\,P^{-1}(t)$ instead of Γ. Here

$$\psi(t) \triangleq \begin{pmatrix} \frac{u(t-k-1)}{P_1} + \hat{\theta}^T(t-1)\,\varphi(t-k-1) \\ \varphi(t-k-1) \end{pmatrix}.$$

□

The intention with the algorithm (2.14) is to exploit the properties of a strictly positive real transfer function in order to establish convergence of $\varepsilon(t)$ to zero. The motivation is the successful use of Lyapunov theory and the Kalman-Yakubovich lemma in continuous time, see Chapter 3. The problems that arise will be discussed next. Let us just briefly comment on the stochastic case. The algorithm given by (2.11), (2.12), and (2.14) cannot be directly applied to the model (2.10), because the C-polynomial is unknown. This implies that the prediction cannot be calculated according to (2.11). An easy modification is to replace C in front of the paranthesis with an a priori estimate of C or even with unity.

Choice of control law

The control law, given in Section 2.1, can be written as

$$u(t) = - P_1(q^{-1}) \, [\theta^T \varphi(t)],$$

where θ is the vector of true parameters. Compare (2.6), (2.8). Any reasonable control law should equal this one when the parameter estimates are correct. Notice that a parameter estimator like (2.14) has the objective to force the prediction error $\varepsilon(t)$ to zero. It would thus be desirable to choose a control such that $\hat{e}_f(t|t-1)$ is equal to zero, because convergence of $e_f(t)$ to zero would then follow from the convergence of $\varepsilon(t)$ to zero, cf. (2.12). This is accomplished by the control law

$$u(t) = - P_1(q^{-1}) \, [\hat{\theta}^T(t+k) \, \varphi(t)]$$

as seen from (2.11). This control law is however noncausal. It is therefore natural to modify it in the following way:

$$u(t) = - P_1(q^{-1}) \, [\hat{\theta}^T(t) \, \varphi(t)]. \tag{2.15}$$

This control law is used in all control schemes of the type considered.

Difficulties with convergence analysis

There are two key problems in the analysis of the schemes of MRAS type described above. The first problem is that the control law (2.15) has to be used if a causal control law is required. This implies that $\hat{e}_f(t|t-1)$ is not equal to zero in the case $k \neq 0$. This in turn means that it is not easy to conclude that $e_f(t)$ tends to zero even if $\varepsilon(t)$ tends to zero.

The second problem is to show that $\varepsilon(t)$ tends to zero. Consider for simplicity the case $k = 0$, which is analogous to the case for continuous time systems, where the pole excess is equal to one, cf. Chapter 3. Then $\varepsilon(t)$ is equal to $e_f(t)$ if the control law (2.15) is used. Contrary to the continuous time case, convergence of $e_f(t)$ to zero cannot be proved straightforwardly. The reason is the following one. If the control law (2.15) is used and it is assumed that $b_0 = 1$, the equation (2.13) can be written

$$\varepsilon(t) = e_f(t) = H(q^{-1}) \cdot q^{-1}[-\tilde{\theta}^T(t)\ \varphi(t)]. \tag{2.16}$$

Here

$$H(q^{-1}) = \frac{Q(q^{-1})}{T(q^{-1})\ A^M(q^{-1})}$$

and

$$\tilde{\theta}(t) = \hat{\theta}(t) - \theta.$$

In continuous time the estimation error $\varepsilon(t)$ is given by

$$\varepsilon(t) = G(p)\ [-\tilde{\theta}^T(t)\ \varphi(t)].$$

Compare Chapter 3. Positive realness of $G(p)$ can be used to prove the convergence of $\varepsilon(t)$ to zero. It is however not possible to use the same arguments in discrete time, because the transfer function $H(q^{-1})\cdot q^{-1}$ can never be made positive real. The difference appears because a discrete time transfer function must contain a feedthrough term to be strictly positive real, whereas a continuous time transfer function may be *strictly* proper. This difficulty is also emphasized in Landau/Bēthoux (1975).

The problem mentioned above and also, in the case $k \neq 0$, the previously mentioned problem to relate convergence of $\varepsilon(t)$ and $e_f(t)$ are closely related to the boundedness of the signals of the closed loop system. This is pointed out in e.g. Ionescu/Monopoli (1977).

2.3. Examples of the general control scheme

Some special cases of the basic control scheme, proposed in the preceeding section, will now be given. Both model reference adaptive systems and self-tuning regulators will be shown to fit into the general description.

EXAMPLE 2.1. *Ionescu's and Monopoli's scheme*

The scheme in Ionescu/Monopoli (1977) is a straightforward translation into discrete time of the continuous time MRAS by Monopoli (1974). It is possible to treat the scheme as a special case of the general algorithm in the following way. Choose the polynomials as

$P_1 = T$ of degree k

P_2 of degree $n-1$

$Q = P = P_1P_2$ of degree $n+k-1$.

The equation (2.6) then transforms into

$$e_f(t) = e(t) = \frac{P_2}{A^M} q^{-(k+1)} \left[b_0 \frac{u(t)}{P_1} + b_0(BR-P_2) \frac{u(t)}{P} + S \frac{y(t)}{P} - \right.$$
$$\left. - \frac{B^M}{P_2} u^M(t) \right], \qquad (2.17)$$

where the disturbance w has been assumed to be zero as in the original presentation. This is the model used by Ionescu and Monopoli and the estimation scheme is similar to the one in (2.14). The polynomial P_2 is chosen to make the transfer function P_2/A^M strictly positive real. Some modifications of the estimation scheme are done to handle the problems discussed in the preceeding section, although no complete solution is presented. The concept of *augmented error*, introduced in Monopoli (1974), is translated into discrete time. It can be shown that the augmented error $\eta(t)$ in the case $k = 0$ is given by

$$\eta(t) = \varepsilon(t) - \frac{P_2}{A^M} [K_\eta \cdot \eta(t) \cdot |\varphi(t-1)|^2],$$

where K_η is a constant. It is shown that $\eta(t)$ tends to zero, but a boundedness assumption is needed to establish convergence of $\varepsilon(t)$ or $e_f(t)$. Finally it should be noted that the polynomials P_1 and P_2 are called Z_f and Z_w in Ionescu/Monopoli (1977). □

EXAMPLE 2.2. *Bénéjean's scheme*

A discrete time MRAS is presented in Bénéjean (1977). It can be shown that the algorithm is very similar to Ionescu's and Monopoli's scheme. The model used by Bénéjean is obtained by reparametrizing (2.17) as follows:

$$e_f(t) = e(t) = \frac{P_2}{A^M} q^{-(k+1)} \Big[b_0 \frac{u(t)-u^M(t)}{P_1} + b_0(BR-P_2) \frac{u(t)-u^M(t)}{P} + \\ + S \frac{y(t)}{P} + (b_0BR - B^MP_1) \frac{u^M(t)}{P} \Big].$$

The estimation algorithm used is similar to the one used by Ionescu and Monopoli. Note that more parameters have to be estimated because of the reparametrization. □

In the two MRAS examples above the natural choice $Q = P$ has been used. This implies that the filtered error $e_f(t)$ equals the error $e(t)$. Another possibility is to choose the polynomials so that the transfer function Q / TA^M becomes very simple. This is done below.

EXAMPLE 2.3. *Self-tuning pole placement algorithm*

A pole placement algorithm with fixed observer polynomial is described in Åström et al. (1978). It can be generated from the general structure in the following way. Choose the polynomials as

$$Q = TA^M$$

$$P = P_1 = P_2 = 1,$$

which means that $e_f(t) = TA^M\, e(t)$. This implies that (2.8) has the simple form

$$e_f(t) = q^{-(k+1)}[b_0\, u(t) + b_0\, \theta^T \varphi(t)], \tag{2.18}$$

where the elements of φ are simply lagged input and output signals. The disturbance has been assumed to be zero. The model (2.18) is used for the self-tuning regulator with a minor modification. The parameters which are estimated by a least squares algorithm are b_0 and $b_0\theta$. Since the last element in θ is $1/b_0$, the effect is that one parameter is known to be equal to one. If θ and φ are redefined not to include the last known element, the equation (2.18) can be written as

$$e_f(t) = TA^M\,[y(t) - y^M(t)] = q^{-(k+1)}[b_0\, u(t) + b_0\, \theta^T \varphi(t)] - TA^M y^M(t),$$

which is the model used. □

In the three examples above the choice of observer polynomial T was made in advance. However, if there is noise of the form given by (2.3), the optimal choice of observer polynomial is T = C, which is unknown. It can then be estimated as described in Section 2.2. Below some schemes of this type will be described.

EXAMPLE 2.4. Åström's and Wittenmark's self-tuning regulator

The basic self-tuning regulator is described in Åström/Wittenmark (1973). It is based on a minimum variance strategy, which minimizes the output variance. This is a special case of the problem considered in Section 2.1 with $A^M = 1$ and $u^M = y^M = 0$. Inserting this into (2.6) and using the polynomials Q = P = 1, the following is obtained:

$$e_f(t) = y(t) = \frac{1}{C}\, q^{-(k+1)}[b_0\, u(t) + b_0(BR-1)\, u(t) + S\, y(t)] + R\, v(t).$$

This model can be written analogously with (2.10) as

$$e_f(t) = y(t) = \frac{1}{C}\, q^{-(k+1)}[b_0\, u(t) + \theta^T \varphi(t)] + R\; v(t) \tag{2.19}$$

and is the basis for the self-tuning regulator. Since C is unknown, the prediction is chosen as in (2.11) with T = C replaced by unity. Compare the discussion in Section 2.2. Hence,

$$\hat{e}_f(t|t-1) = \hat{y}(t|t-1) = \hat{b}_0(t-1)u(t-k-1) + \hat{\theta}^T(t-1)\varphi(t-k-1). \qquad (2.20)$$

The fact that C is included in (2.19) but not in (2.20) makes it somewhat unexpected that the algorithm really converges to the optimal minimum variance regulator. It is shown in Ljung (1977a) that the scheme (with a stochastic approximation estimation algorithm) converges if 1/C is strictly positive real. If instead a least squares estimation algorithm is used, convergence holds if 1/C - 1/2 is SPR. The condition on 1/C and its relation to the positive real condition for MRAS will be further examined in the following section. □

EXAMPLE 2.5. *Clarke's and Gawthrop's self-tuning controller*

Clarke and Gawthrop (1975) consider a 'generalized output'

$$\phi(t) = P(q^{-1})y(t) + Q(q^{-1})u(t-k-1) - R(q^{-1})u^M(t-k-1)$$

and applies the basic self-tuning regulator to the system generating this output. It is possible to treat the algorithm within the general structure in the special case Q = 0 in their notation. Thus change the notation into:

$$\phi(t) = A^M(q^{-1})y(t) - q^{-(k+1)}B^M(q^{-1})u^M(t).$$

Then it follows that $\phi(t)$ equals $e_f(t) = A^M e(t)$ if P = 1 and $Q = A^M$. If the noise is given by (2.3) and T is chosen to be equal to C, the equation (2.6) can be written as

$$e_f(t) = \frac{1}{C} q^{-(k+1)}[b_0 u(t) + b_0(BR-1)u(t) + Sy(t) - CB^M u^M(t)] + Rv(t).$$

This is the model used in the self-tuning controller. The fact that the first parameter in C is known to be unity is exploited. The prediction is calculated as in Example 2.4, i.e. C in front of the parenthesis is replaced by unity. The estimation scheme is a least squares algorithm. □

2.4. The positive real condition

A special model structure and a specific estimation scheme were described in Section 2.2. The structure was obtained from an analogy with the model reference adaptive systems in continuous time. The intention was to use the properties of positive real transfer functions to establish convergence. It was noted in Example 2.4 that a positive real condition also appears in the analysis of a self-tuning regulator in the presense of noise. The relations between the conditions in the two cases will be treated below.

First consider the deterministic design case and for simplicity assume that $k = 0$ and $b_0 = 1$. If the control law (2.15) is used, we have from (2.16)

$$\varepsilon(t) = -H(q^{-1})[\tilde{\theta}^T(t-1)\varphi(t-1)]. \tag{2.21}$$

We want to show in a simple way that a positive real condition really appears in the analysis in a natural way. To do so, assume that a modified version of the parameter updating (2.14) is used:

$$\hat{\theta}(t) = \hat{\theta}(t-1) + \frac{\varphi(t-1)}{|\varphi(t-1)|^2}\varepsilon(t). \tag{2.22}$$

This algorithm is similar to stochastic approximation schemes and is used in e.g. Ionescu/Monopoli (1977).

Subtract the true parameter vector θ from both sides, multiply from the left by the transpose and use (2.21) to get

$$|\tilde{\theta}(t)|^2 = |\tilde{\theta}(t-1)|^2 + 2\,\frac{\tilde{\theta}^T(t-1)\varphi(t-1)}{|\varphi(t-1)|^2}\,\varepsilon(t) + \frac{\varepsilon^2(t)}{|\varphi(t-1)|^2} =$$

$$= |\tilde{\theta}(t-1)|^2 - 2\,\frac{\varepsilon(t)\left(\frac{\varepsilon(t)}{H(q^{-1})}\right)}{|\varphi(t-1)|^2} + \frac{\varepsilon^2(t)}{|\varphi(t-1)|^2} =$$

$$= |\tilde{\theta}(t-1)|^2 - 2\,\frac{\varepsilon(t)[(1/H - 1/2)\varepsilon(t)]}{|\varphi(t-1)|^2}. \tag{2.23}$$

It can be seen that the positive real condition enters in a natural way. If $1/H - 1/2$ is positive real, the parameter error will eventually decrease. Moreover, $\varepsilon(t) / |\varphi(t-1)|$ tends to zero if $1/H - 1/2$ is SPR. It should be noted that the boundedness condition mentioned in Section 2.2 appears because (2.23) only proves convergence of $\varepsilon(t) / |\varphi(t-1)|$.

It is straightforward to show that the positive real condition can be avoided. Thus, let $\overline{x}$ denote the signal obtained by filtering x by Q/TA^M and rewrite (2.8) as

$$e_f(t) = q^{-1}\left[\frac{\overline{u}(t)}{P_1(q^{-1})} + \theta^T \overline{\varphi}(t)\right], \tag{2.24}$$

where the same assumptions as above are used. Now consider this as being the model instead of (2.8). The prediction (2.11) is then replaced by

$$\hat{e}_f(t|t-1) = \frac{\overline{u}(t-1)}{P_1} + \hat{\theta}^T(t-1)\, \overline{\varphi}(t-1),$$

which is different from (2.11) because $\hat{\theta}(t)$ is timevarying. Instead of (2.21) we then have

$$\varepsilon(t) = - \tilde{\theta}^T(t-1)\, \overline{\varphi}(t-1).$$

If the parameter updating (2.22) is replaced by

$$\hat{\theta}(t) = \hat{\theta}(t-1) + \frac{\overline{\varphi}(t-1)}{|\overline{\varphi}(t-1)|^2}\, \varepsilon(t), \tag{2.25}$$

the following is obtained:

$$|\tilde{\theta}(t)|^2 = |\tilde{\theta}(t-1)|^2 + 2\, \frac{\tilde{\theta}^T(t-1)\, \overline{\varphi}(t-1)}{|\overline{\varphi}(t-1)|^2}\, \varepsilon(t) + \frac{\varepsilon^2(t)}{|\overline{\varphi}(t-1)|^2} =$$

$$= |\tilde{\theta}(t-1)|^2 - \frac{\varepsilon^2(t)}{|\overline{\varphi}(t-1)|^2}\, .$$

It thus follows that $\varepsilon(t) / |\overline{\varphi}(t-1)|$ tends to zero without any positive real condition. Of course the boundedness of the closed loop signals mentioned in Section 2.2 is still a problem. The conclusion is that it is possible to eliminate the positive real condition in the deterministic design case if a modified estimation scheme is used.

Now consider the stochastic design, where the observer polynomial C is estimated. The transfer function $H(q^{-1})$, which was previously known, now contains the unknown C-polynomial. This implies that the filtering in (2.24) and (2.25) cannot be done with the true C-polynomial. The positive real condition then enters in the same way as in Example 2.4. The positive real condition on $H(q^{-1}) = 1/C(q^{-1})$ and a boundedness condition are in fact sufficient to assure convergence for the self--tuning regulator in Example 2.4, see Ljung (1977a). A natural modification in order to weaken the condition on C is to filter with $1/\hat{C}(t)$, where $\hat{C}(t)$ is the timevarying estimate of C. This is further discussed in Ljung (1977a).

The conclusion of the discussion above is that the positive real condition, which appears in the analysis of both deterministic MRAS and stochastic STR, are of a similar technical nature. There is, however, an important difference. The condition can be eliminated for the deterministic case by choosing another estimation algorithm, which includes filtering by the transfer function $H(q^{-1})$. In the stochastic case, the positive real condition is not possible to be dispensed with in the same way, because the filter is unknown.

3. UNIFIED DESCRIPTION OF CONTINUOUS TIME CONTROLLERS

The MRAS schemes were originally developed in continuous time. The solution for the problem with output feedback was given in Gilbart et al. (1970) for the easy case with pole excess of the plant equal to one or two. The pole excess is defined as the difference between the number of poles and the number of zeros. The solution was reformulated in a nice way by Monopoli (1973). Monopoli (1974) introduced the concept of *augmented error* to treat the general case. Similar schemes are proposed by Bénéjean (1977), Feuer/Morse (1977), and Narendra/Valavani (1977).

Self-tuning regulators have not been formulated in continuous time before. Yet, it is of interest to relate the MRAS philosophy and the separation idea behind the STR in continuous time too. In this chapter some MRAS schemes will be derived in a unified manner from the STR point of view. The development gives a new interpretation of the augmented error, introduced by Monopoli. Some problems in the analysis are also pointed out and the positive real condition for MRAS is examined. It is shown that the condition can be dispensed with. It should be noted that the treatment of the continuous time schemes is not as complete as for discrete time. Only the deterministic design is considered. It should, however, be possible to carry through a development, analogous with discrete time, in the stochastic design case too.

3.1. Design method for known plants

Before a unified description of several algorithms is given, the known parameter case has to be considered. A design scheme, which includes interesting special cases, will be described in this section. It is analogous to the discrete time procedure in Section 2.1. The scheme is given in Åström (1976) and special cases are treated in e.g. Narendra/Valavani (1977), and Bénéjean (1977).

The plant is assumed to satisfy the differential equation

$$y(t) = \frac{b_0 B(p)}{A(p)} u(t) = \frac{b_0(p^m + b_1 p^{m-1} + \ldots + b_m)}{p^n + a_1 p^{n-1} + \ldots + a_n} u(t), \tag{3.1}$$

where p denotes the differential operator.

REMARK 1

It is assumed that there is no disturbance. It is convenient to make this assumption in this chapter, because the design is deterministic. Disturbances will, however, be introduced in the stability analysis in Chapter 5. □

REMARK 2

The parameter b_0 is not included in the B-polynomial, because it will be treated in a special way in the estimation part of the adaptive controller in the next section. Compare Chapter 2. □

The objective of the controller is to make the closed-loop transfer operator equal to a reference model transfer operator, given by

$$y^M(t) = \frac{B^M(p)}{A^M(p)} u^M(t) = \frac{b_0^M p^m + \ldots + b_m^M}{p^n + a_1^M p^{n-1} + \ldots + a_n^M} u^M(t). \tag{3.2}$$

Here $y^M(t)$ is the desired output of the closed loop system and $u^M(t)$ is the command input. It is seen that the pole excess of the reference model is greater than or equal to the pole excess of the plant. This assumption is made to avoid differentiators in the control law.

Analogous to the discrete time case, a controller structure as shown in Fig. 3.1 will be considered. The controller polynomials R, S, and T are polynomials in the differential operator p. The configuration is motivated in e.g. Åström (1976). As in the discrete time case it is related to a solution with Kalman filter and state estimate feedback. The T-polynomial can be interpreted as an observer polynomial. Also note that the B-polynomial is cancelled, restricting the design method to minimum phase systems.

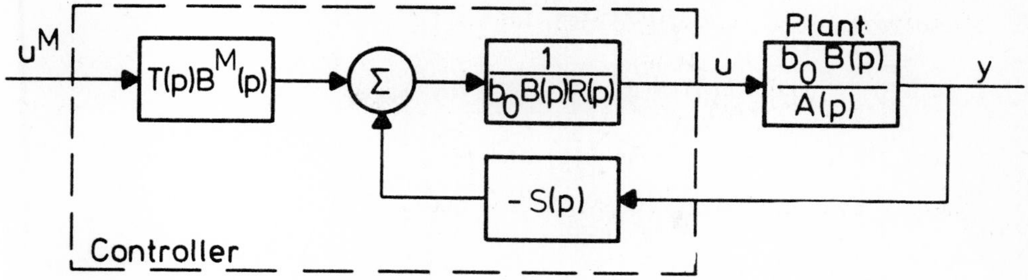

Figure 3.1. Controller configuration.

The desired closed-loop transfer function is obtained if the polynomials R, S, and T are chosen to satisfy the equation

$$\frac{B^M(p)}{A^M(p)} = \frac{b_0\ B(p)\ T(p)\ B^M(p)}{A(p)\ b_0\ B(p)\ R(p) + b_0\ B(p)\ S(p)}$$

or, equivalently,

$$T(p)\ A^M(p) = A(p)\ R(p) + S(p). \tag{3.3}$$

The observer polynomial T(p) is cancelled in the closed-loop transfer function. If the effects of initial values are neglected, it can therefore be chosen arbitrarily. When T(p) has been determined, the equation (3.3) has many solutions S(p) and R(p). It will, however, be assumed that the degree of S(p) is less than or equal to n-1, which assures that the equation has a unique solution, Åström (1976). Since the polynomials A(p) and $A^M(p)$ both have degree n, T(p) and R(p) will have the same degree n_T. In order to assure that the control law does not contain any derivatives of the output, n_T is chosen greater than or equal to n-m-1. Furthermore, R and T are scaled so that they are monic.

In summary then, the design scheme consists of the following steps:

1) Choose the monic polynomial T(p)

$$T(p) = p^{n_T} + t_1\ p^{n_T-1} + \ldots + t_{n_T}, \quad n_T \geq n-m-1.$$

2) Solve the equation

$$T(p)\, A^M(p) = A(p)\, R(p) + S(p)$$

for the unique solutions R(p) and S(p), defined by

$$S(p) = s_0\, p^{n-1} + \ldots + s_{n-1}$$

$$R(p) = p^{n_T} + r_1\, p^{n_T-1} + \ldots + r_{n_T}.$$

The first step, the choice of T(p) (including its degree) does not affect the closed-loop transfer function. However, it is of importance for the transient properties and the effect of disturbances as was seen in Chapter 2. The importance of the noise colour for the choice of observer will, however, not influence the discussion in this chapter, since only the deterministic design case is considered.

3.2. Class of adaptive controllers

The idea behind the self-tuning regulators will be used in this section to define a general class of adaptive regulators. These regulators will be adaptive versions of the controller described in Section 3.1. The class of algorithms will later be shown to include several MRAS schemes as special cases.

The plant is still assumed to satisfy (3.1). The following assumptions are also introduced.

A1) The degrees n and m are known and $m \leq n - 1$.

A2) The parameter b_0 is nonzero and its sign is known. Without loss of generality b_0 is assumed to be positive.

A3) The plant is minimum phase.

REMARK

Notice that it is sufficient to know the pole excess and an upper bound on the number of poles to write the differential equation in the form of (3.1) with known n and m. Knowledge of the pole excess is the counterpart of the discrete time condition, that the time delay is known, cf. Chapter 2. The minimum phase assumption was discussed in Section 3.1. □

The desired closed-loop transfer function is given by (3.2). The first step in the development is to use the results in Section 3.1 to obtain a model, expressed in the unknown controller parameters. Compare with Section 2.2.

The polynomial identity (3.3) and the equations (3.1) and (3.2) are used to get the following expression for the error $e(t) = y(t) - y^M(t)$:

$$TA^M e(t) = TA^M y(t) - TA^M y^M(t) = (AR + S)\, y(t) - TA^M y^M(t) =$$

$$= b_0 BRu(t) + Sy(t) - TB^M u^M(t). \tag{3.4}$$

Let $P_1(p)$, $P_2(p)$, and $Q(p)$ be stable, monic polynomials of degree $n - m - 1$, $m + n_T$, and $n + n_T - 1$ respectively, and let $P(p)$ be given by

$$P(p) = P_1(p)P_2(p).$$

Define the filtered error

$$e_f(t) = \frac{Q(p)}{P(p)}\, e(t),$$

which thus is a known quantity. Using (3.4), $e_f(t)$ can be written as

$$e_f(t) = \frac{Q}{TA^M}\left[\frac{b_0 BR}{P}\, u(t) + \frac{S}{P}\, y(t) - \frac{TB^M}{P}\, u^M(t)\right] =$$

$$= \frac{Q}{TA^M}\left[b_0 \frac{u(t)}{P_1} + b_0(BR - P_2)\frac{u(t)}{P} + S\frac{y(t)}{P} - \frac{TB^M}{P}\, u^M(t)\right]. \tag{3.5}$$

REMARK

The motive to introduce the polynomials Q and P and the filtered error is the flexibility obtained. Different choices of polynomials will be seen to generate different MRAS schemes in the examples in the next section. Also compare with Chapter 2. It should also be noted that

Q and P could be chosen as rational functions, but this generalization will not be considered here. □

Let θ be a vector containing the unknown parameters of the polynomials $BR - P_2$ (degree $m + n_T - 1$) and S/b_0 (degree $n - 1$) and the constant $1/b_0$ as the last element. Note that the vector θ contains the parameters of the controller, described in Section 3.1. Furthermore, define the vector

$$\varphi^T(t) = \left[\frac{p^{m+n_T-1}}{P} u(t), \ldots, \frac{1}{P} u(t), \frac{p^{n-1}}{P} y(t), \ldots, \frac{1}{P} y(t), -\frac{TB^M}{P} u^M(t)\right]. \tag{3.6}$$

It is then possible to rewrite the expression (3.5) for the filtered error $e_f(t)$ as

$$e_f(t) = \frac{Q}{TA^M}\left[b_0 \frac{u(t)}{P_1} + b_0\, \theta^T\, \varphi(t)\right]. \tag{3.7}$$

This model provides the starting-point for a class of adaptive controllers as in discrete time. Note that $e_f(t)$ is still a known quantity. As before, there is a lot of freedom when specifying the estimation algorithm and the control law. The development done so far thus proposes a class of adaptive controllers, defined in two steps.

BASIC CONTROL SCHEME

- o Estimate the unknown parameters b_0 and θ (or some combination of these) in the model (3.7).
- o Use these estimates to determine the control signal.

To make the discussion easier, it is convenient to specify a particular estimation algorithm as was done in discrete time.

A special parameter estimator

A specific structure of the estimation part will be discussed below. It is of special interest because many MRAS schemes use this structure.

It is analogous to the special configuration for discrete time controllers discussed in Chapter 2.

Using the model (3.7), an estimate of $e_f(t)$ is defined as

$$\hat{e}_f(t) = \frac{Q}{TA^M}\left[\hat{b}_0(t)\,\frac{u(t)}{P_1} + \hat{b}_0(t)\,\hat{\theta}^T(t)\,\varphi(t)\right], \qquad (3.8)$$

where $\hat{b}_0(t)$ and $\hat{\theta}(t)$ are estimates of b_0 and θ. Define the difference between the filtered error and its estimate as

$$\varepsilon(t) = e_f(t) - \hat{e}_f(t). \qquad (3.9)$$

The following equation is then obtained for $\varepsilon(t)$:

$$\varepsilon(t) = \frac{Q}{TA^M}\left[[b_0-\hat{b}_0(t)]\left(\frac{u(t)}{P_1} + \hat{\theta}^T(t)\,\varphi(t)\right) + b_0[\theta - \hat{\theta}(t)]^T\,\varphi(t)\right]. \qquad (3.10)$$

The following parameter updating is used in the constant gain case:

$$\begin{pmatrix} \dot{\hat{b}}_0(t) \\ \dot{\hat{\theta}}(t) \end{pmatrix} = \Gamma \begin{pmatrix} \frac{u(t)}{P_1} + \hat{\theta}^T(t)\,\varphi(t) \\ \varphi(t) \end{pmatrix} \varepsilon(t), \qquad (3.11)$$

where Γ is a constant, positive definite matrix.

REMARK

It is possible to define variants of the algorithm (3.11) with Γ replaced by some timevarying gain. These schemes can be defined analogously with the discrete time case and the details are not given.

□

If the parameter updating (3.11) is used and the transfer function Q/TA^M is strictly positive real, it is possible to apply Lyapunov theory and the Kalman-Yakubovich lemma to assure that $\varepsilon(t)$ tends to zero, provided that the closed-loop signals are bounded. See e.g. Monopoli (1973). Note that the estimation scheme (3.11) was the motivation for the scheme (2.14) considered in Chapter 2. Also note that Q/TA^M can always be made strictly positive real by choosing Q appropriately, because T and A^M are known and the degree of Q is one less than the degree of TA^M.

The estimation part of the controller with MRAS structure is defined by equations (3.8), (3.9), and (3.11). Note that $e_f(t)$ is known. So far the second part of the controller - the control law - has not been discussed. This will be done next.

Choice of control law

The choice of control law contains one difficulty. It is natural to determine the control signal so that the estimate of the error, i.e. $\hat{e}_f(t)$, is equal to zero. According to equation (3.8) this means that

$$u(t) = - P_1(p) [\hat{\theta}^T(t) \varphi(t)]. \tag{3.12}$$

This control law is identical to the one described in Section 3.1 if $\hat{\theta}(t)$ is equal to the true parameter vector θ in (3.7). This can be seen from (3.5).

The control law, however, uses derivatives of the parameter estimates, except for the trivial case when $m = n - 1$, i.e. the pole excess is equal to one. In this case P_1 is a constant. Since $\hat{\theta}(t)$ is in general obtained by integration of known signals as in (3.11), it is in fact possible to use (3.12) without differentiators also in the case $m = n - 2$.

However, in the general case the control law must be modified in order not to include differentiators. Compare the discussion of the control law in the case $k \neq 0$ in Section 2.2. There are different solutions proposed in the literature. For example, Monopoli (1974) chooses a control signal which corresponds to the choice

$$u(t) = - \hat{\theta}^T(t) [P_1(p) \varphi(t)]. \tag{3.13}$$

It is clear that the control law (3.13) is asymptotically equivalent to the control law (3.12). Note that it follows from the definition of $\varphi(t)$ that $P_1(p)\varphi(t)$ contains filtered input, output and reference signals without any derivatives. The choice (3.13) does not guarantee that $\hat{e}_f(t) = 0$, and it remains to conclude that $e_f(t)$ tends to zero from the fact that $\varepsilon(t) = e_f(t) - \hat{e}_f(t)$ tends to zero. This problem is closely related to the problem of boundedness of the closed-loop signals. Compare with the discussion in Section 2.2.

3.3. Examples of the general control scheme

Some special cases of the procedure proposed in Section 3.2 will now be given. Several MRAS schemes proposed in the literature will be shown to fit into the general algorithm. As a side result, the *augmented error* introduced by Monopoli is given a new interpretation. A new algorithm is also given to illustrate the large number of schemes that are possible to derive from the general algorithm.

EXAMPLE 3.1. Monopoli's scheme

The scheme by Monopoli (1974) has been frequently discussed, because it was an attempt to solve the adaptive control problem when the pole excess of the plant is greater than two. Monopoli introduced the concept of *augmented error*, motivated by the results on adaptive observers. The scheme will be described in some detail in order to show the interpretation of the augmented error. To be consistent with the preceeding section, the notation is different from Monopoli's. A cross reference table between the notations is given in Table 3.1.

In summary, Monopoli's scheme is as follows. Monic polynomials D_w (degree $n-1$) and D_f (degree $n-m-1$) are chosen. Furthermore, the polynomials D (degree $n-2$), F (degree $n-m-2$), and G (degree $n-1$) are solved from the identities

$$D_w = BD_f + D/b_0$$

$$(A - A^M)\, D_f = AF + G.$$

With these polynomials, $e(t) = y(t) - y^M(t)$ can be written as

Table 3.1. Present notation compared to Monopoli's

present	Monopoli's
$y(t)$	$x(t)$
$y^M(t)$	$x_m(t)$
$u^M(t)$	$r^1(t)$
$B^M(p)u^M(t)$	$r(t)$
$e(t)$	$-e(t)$
$e_1(t)$	$y(t)$
$\eta(t)$	$-\eta(t)$
$A(p)$	$D_p(p)$
$b_0B(p)$	$D_u(p)$
$A^M(p)$	$D_m(p)$
$B^M(p)$	$D_r(p)$
$-D(p)$	$A(p)$
$G(p)$	$B(p)$
$b_0B(p)F(p)$	$C(p)$

$$e(t) = \frac{D_w}{A^M}\left[b_0 \frac{u(t)}{D_f} - b_0(D/b_0 + BF)\frac{u(t)}{D_fD_w} - G\frac{y(t)}{D_fD_w} - \frac{B^M}{D_w}u^M(t)\right] \triangleq$$

$$\triangleq \frac{D_w}{A^M}\left[b_0 \frac{u(t)}{D_f} + b_0\, \theta^T \varphi(t)\right], \tag{3.14}$$

where θ and φ are defined as in the derivation of the controller in Section 3.2.

The augmented error $\eta(t)$ is defined as

$$\eta(t) = e(t) - e_1(t) \tag{3.15}$$

where

$$e_1(t) = \frac{D_w(p)}{A^M(p)}\,[\hat{b}_0(t)\, w_1(t)] \tag{3.16}$$

and the auxiliary signal $w_1(t)$ is determined so that

$$\frac{u(t)}{D_f(p)} + \hat{\theta}^T(t)\,\varphi(t) = w_1(t). \tag{3.17}$$

Here $\hat{b}_0(t)$ and $\hat{\theta}(t)$ denote estimates at time t of b_0 and θ. If the closed-loop signals are bounded, the positive realness of D_w/A^M can be shown to assure the convergence of the augmented error to zero, see Monopoli (1974). However, even if $\eta(t)$ tends to zero, it does not follow that e(t) tends to zero, which is the primary goal. Monopoli makes this conclusion under the crucial boundedness assumption. Compare the discussion in Section 3.2.

It is easy to give an interpretation of the augmented error from the equations given above. Thus, if Equation (3.17) is inserted into Equation (3.16), the following is obtained:

$$e_1(t) = \frac{D_w(p)}{A^M(p)} \left[\hat{b}_0(t)\left(\frac{u(t)}{D_f(p)} + \hat{\theta}^T(t)\ \varphi(t)\right)\right].$$

Compare this with the identity (3.14). The conclusion is that

$$e_1(t) = \hat{e}(t),$$

where $\hat{e}(t)$ is an estimate of e(t) using the model (3.14) with the latest available parameter estimates. From equation (3.15) it then follows that the augmented error η is simply the estimation error, i.e. the difference between e(t) and its estimate $\hat{e}(t)$. This quantity is denoted $\varepsilon(t)$ in the preceeding section.

It is straightforward to show that the scheme by Monopoli is a special case of the general algorithm in Section 3.2. Thus, it is possible to verify that the expression (3.14) coincides with (3.5) if the degree of T, n_T, is chosen to be $n - m - 1$. The polynomials are related as follows:

$$Q = P$$

$$D_f = P_1 = T$$

$$D_w = P_2$$

$$D = b_0(P_2 - BP_1)$$

$$F = P_1 - R$$

$$G = -S.$$

The filtered error is thus equal to the error itself. Furthermore, Monopoli chooses the control signal according to (3.13). It can be seen from (3.17) that the control law (3.12) corresponds to the choice $w_1(t) = 0$. If $n - m \leqslant 2$ it is thus possible to set the extra signal w_1 to zero and this means that the augmented error $\eta(t)$ is simply equal to the error $e(t)$. □

EXAMPLE 3.2. Bênêjean's scheme

The scheme is presented in Bênêjean (1977) and can be shown to be a variant of Monopoli's. The model used is obtained from Monopoli's after a reparametrization:

$$e_f(t) = \frac{Q}{TA^M}\left[b_0 \frac{u(t) - u^M(t)}{P_1} + b_0(BR - P_2)\frac{u(t) - u^M(t)}{P} + S\frac{y(t)}{P} - \right.$$

$$\left. - (TB^M - b_0 BR)\frac{u^M(t)}{P}\right].$$

The choices of polynomials are identical to Monopoli's and so are the estimation algorithm and the choice of control law. Note that more parameters have to be estimated because of the reparametrization.

□

EXAMPLE 3.3. Feuer's and Morse's scheme

The scheme is given in Feuer/Morse (1977). A minor change of the design method described in Section 3.1 will be needed in order to treat the algorithm within the general framework. To this end, write the reference model transfer function as

$$\frac{B^M(p)}{A^M(p)} = \frac{1}{\gamma_0(p)\ \gamma_1(p)}\ h(p),$$

where $\gamma_0(p)$ and $\gamma_1(p)$ are monic polynomials of degree 1 and $n - m - 1$ respectively. The degree of $\gamma_0\gamma_1$ is thus equal to the pole excess of the plant and $h(p)$ is a proper transfer operator. Now, consider $h(p)u^M(t)$ as being the input to the reference model with transfer function $1/\gamma_0\gamma_1$. The effect is that the development proceeds as if $B^M = 1$ and $A^M = \gamma_0\gamma_1$. The modification necessary is seen from the identity corresponding to Equation (3.3), i.e.

$$T(p)\ \gamma_0(p)\ \gamma_1(p) = A(p)\ R(p) + S(p).$$

If n_T is chosen to be equal to n, it follows that R(p) has the same degree as $\gamma_0\gamma_1$, i.e. $n - m$. This is different from the other schemes. The control law for the known parameter case now is

$$b_0B(p)\ R(p)\ u(t) = T(p)\ h(p)\ u^M(t) - S(p)\ y(t)$$

which is identical to the one in Figure 3.1 with $B^M = 1$ and u^M replaced by $h(p)\ u^M$. With the above modifications, the equation (3.5) becomes

$$e_f(t) = \frac{Q}{T\gamma_0\gamma_1}\left[b_0\ \frac{u(t)}{P_1} + b_0(BR - P_2)\ \frac{u(t)}{P} + S\ \frac{y(t)}{P} - \frac{T}{P}\ h\ u^M(t)\right] \tag{3.18}$$

where Q and P now should be of degree $n_T + n - m - 1$, because A^M has been replaced by $\gamma_0\gamma_1$.

Now choose the polynomials according to

$$P_1 = \gamma_1$$

$$P_2 = T$$

$$Q = P = P_1P_2.$$

Then (3.18) transforms to

$$e(t) = \frac{1}{\gamma_0}\left[b_0\ \frac{u(t)}{\gamma_1} + b_0(BR - T)\ \frac{u(t)}{\gamma_1 T} + S\ \frac{y(t)}{\gamma_1 T} - \frac{h}{\gamma_1}\ u^M(t)\right]$$

which is the model used by Feuer and Morse. The estimation algorithm is the ordinary MRAS scheme. The control law is, however, a special and complicated one, derived to obtain stability of the closed loop. Compare the discussion in Section 3.2. □

EXAMPLE 3.4. Narendra's and Valavani's scheme

The scheme is described in Narendra/Valavani (1977). By choosing the observer order n_T to be equal to $n - m - 1$ and the polynomials according to

$$P_1 = L$$

$$P_2 = TB^M/b_0^M$$

$$Q = P = P_1P_2,$$

the equation (3.5) transforms into

$$e(t) = \frac{B^M L}{b_0^M A^M}\left[b_0 \frac{u(t)}{L} + b_0(BR - TB^M/b_0^M)\frac{u(t)}{LTB^M/b_0^M} + \right.$$

$$\left. + S\frac{y(t)}{LTB^M/b_0^M} - \frac{b_0^M}{L} u^M(t)\right].$$

This is the model used and the parameter estimation is analogous to the other MRAS described. The polynomial L is chosen to make the transfer function $B^M L/b_0^M A^M$ strictly positive real. □

The above four examples describe algorithms that are proposed in the literature. However, the general algorithm presented in Section 3.2 has a lot of freedom in the choices of polynomials, estimation algorithm etc. Thus, many algorithms can easily be generated. A specific algorithm will be given below, which does not require the positive real condition. Further comments on the positive real condition are given in the following section.

EXAMPLE 3.5. A new algorithm

When using the model (3.5) and the ordinary MRAS estimation scheme, the positive real condition on Q/TA^M enters. A modification of the polynomial degrees, so that degree $(P_1) = n - m$ and degree (Q) = degree $(P) = n + n_T$, makes it very natural to choose

$$Q = P = TA^M.$$

The transfer function $Q/TA^M = 1$ is automatically strictly positive real. However, since the degree of P_1 is $n - m$, it is possible to set $\hat{e}_f(t)$ to zero by the control law only in the case $n - m = 1$. Compare the discussion in Section 3.2. The ordinary MRAS estimation scheme of course can be used in this case too. □

3.4. The positive real condition

The positive real condition has been seen to be an essential condition in order to guarantee convergence of the estimation error. The condition has been an attribute of the MRAS algorithms ever since Parks (1966) introduced the idea. However, it has been demonstrated in Example 3.5 in the preceeding section that the condition can be removed if the polynomials Q and P are chosen in a special way. It is, in fact, possible to use a slightly different estimation algorithm in all the MRAS described, and eliminate the positive real condition in all cases discussed.

Thus, write (3.7) as

$$e_f(t) = b_0 \frac{\overline{u}(t)}{P_1} + b_0 \theta^T \overline{\varphi}(t),$$

where '$\overline{}$' denotes filtering by Q/TA^M. Let the estimate $\hat{e}_f(t)$ be given by

$$\hat{e}_f(t) = \hat{b}_0(t) \frac{\overline{u}(t)}{P_1} + \hat{b}_0(t) \hat{\theta}^T(t) \overline{\varphi}(t)$$

instead of (3.8). Introduce

$$\tilde{b}_0(t) = \hat{b}_0(t) - b_0$$

$$\tilde{\theta}(t) = \hat{\theta}(t) - \theta.$$

The estimation error $\varepsilon(t)$ in (3.9) satisfies the equation

$$\varepsilon(t) = -\tilde{b}_0(t) \left(\frac{\overline{u}(t)}{P_1} + \hat{\theta}^T(t) \overline{\varphi}(t)\right) - b_0 \tilde{\theta}^T(t) \overline{\varphi}(t).$$

Now choose $\varepsilon^2(t)$ as a criterion. Regarding it as a function of $\tilde{b}_0$ and $\tilde{\theta}$, we have

$$\frac{\partial \varepsilon^2(t)}{\partial \tilde{b}_0} = -2\varepsilon(t) \left(\frac{\overline{u}(t)}{P_1} + \hat{\theta}^T(t) \overline{\varphi}(t)\right)$$

$$\frac{\partial \varepsilon^2(t)}{\partial \tilde{\theta}} = -2\varepsilon(t)\, b_0 \overline{\varphi}(t).$$

It is natural to make the parameter adjustment in a modified steepest descent direction, i.e.

$$\begin{cases} \dot{\tilde{b}}_0(t) = \dfrac{1}{r_0}\left(\dfrac{\overline{u(t)}}{P_1} + \hat{\theta}^T(t)\,\overline{\varphi}(t)\right)\varepsilon(t), & r_0 \text{ positive constant} \\ \dot{\tilde{\theta}}(t) = \Gamma^{-1}\,\overline{\varphi}(t)\,\varepsilon(t), & \Gamma \text{ positive definite.} \end{cases}$$

It is possible to verify that this estimation scheme has the desired stability property. Choose the Lyapunov function

$$V(t) = r_0\tilde{b}_0^2(t) + b_0\,\tilde{\theta}^T(t)\,\Gamma\,\tilde{\theta}(t).$$

Its derivative becomes

$$\dot{V}(t) = 2r_0\tilde{b}_0(t)\,\dot{\tilde{b}}_0(t) + 2b_0\tilde{\theta}^T(t)\,\Gamma\,\dot{\tilde{\theta}}(t) =$$

$$= 2\tilde{b}_0(t)\left(\frac{\overline{u(t)}}{P_1} + \hat{\theta}^T(t)\,\overline{\varphi}(t)\right)\varepsilon(t) + 2b_0\tilde{\theta}^T(t)\,\overline{\varphi}(t)\,\varepsilon(t) = -\,2\varepsilon^2(t)$$

and it follows under mild conditions that $\varepsilon(t)$ tends to zero. The details will be considered in Chapter 5.

The conclusion is that by modifying the estimation part, it is possible to eliminate the positive real condition in all the described MRAS. It should, however, be noted that the same situation occurs as in Example 3.5. It is possible to have $\hat{e}_f(t) = 0$ without differentiators only in the case $n - m = 1$.

4. STABILITY OF DISCRETE TIME CONTROLLERS

Stability of the closed loop system is fundamental in applications of adaptive control. Stability is also essential in most theoretical studies of model reference adaptive systems and self-tuning regulators. The problems which appear for discrete time MRAS were discussed in Section 2.2. It was shown that it is difficult to relate convergence of the filtered error $e_f(t)$ and its prediction error $\varepsilon(t)$ in the general case $k \neq 0$. Moreover, even if $k = 0$ the convergence problem could not readily be solved because boundedness of the closed loop signals was not easy to prove. These problems have been emphasized in e.g. Landau/Bêthoux (1975) and Ionescu/Monopoli (1977). Recently, a solution in the disturbance-free case was given by Goodwin et al. (1978a).

The stability problem also appears for the self-tuning regulators, both in practice and in theory. The convergence results mentioned in Chapter 2 require that the estimates and the input and output signals belong to a bounded area infinitely often, see Ljung (1977a). Similar results by Goodwin et al. (1978b) do not, however, require the stability assumption. Stability in sample mean square sense has been considered by Ljung/Wittenmark (1976) and Gawthrop (1978).

The stability problem can be approached in several different ways. Local stability results are given by e.g. Feuer/Morse (1978). This technique is of limited interest because it tells little about the global properties. The global stability properties are much more difficult to investigate. One possibility is to apply Lyapunov theory, but the technique suffers from the difficulty to find a suitable Lyapunov function. This approach has been used in Feuer/Morse (1977) to design a globally stable MRAS in continuous time. The adaptive regulator obtained in this way is unfortunately very complicated.

An alternative to the Lyapunov function approach is to analyse the systems directly. In fact, the partitioning of the schemes into estimation and control parts suggests the following intuitive argument. Consider a situation when the parameter estimates would give an unstable closed-loop system. The plant output increases and after some time the signals are so large that the disturbances become insignificant. The estimates then tend to be accurate and consequently give a stable closed-loop. The plant output thus decreases again.

There are, however, some shortcomings in the heuristic argument given above. Firstly, it is not obvious that all parameter estimates become accurate when the signal amplitudes are growing. It might happen that only some parameter combination is accurately estimated but that the estimates which cause the instability are still poor. Secondly, it takes some time for the estimates to become good, even if the signals are very large. The reasoning above will thus not be valid if the output increases very fast or if the parameter adjustment is very slow.

In this chapter some stability results will be given for the general adaptive algorithm described in Chapter 2. The heuristic discussion given above will be converted into formal proofs. In particular, the assumptions needed to overcome the difficulties mentioned above will be discussed. Uniform boundedness of the closed-loop signals, i.e. L^{∞}-stability, will be considered. It is then natural to assume that the inputs to the overall system, i.e. the command input u^M and the disturbance w, are bounded. If it is not desirable to introduce this assumption, some other stability concept could be considered, e.g. stability in mean square as in Ljung/Wittenmark (1976).

The algorithms treated are based on either deterministic or stochastic design, see Chapter 2. The estimation schemes used are stochastic approximation and least squares algorithms. The main effort has been devoted to the stochastic approximation case. For the least squares version only partial results are given. The analysis is carried out mainly for models where the parameters enter bilinearly as in (2.8). This structure simplifies the stability analysis, but the significance of the product structure is still an open problem.

The algorithms under consideration are briefly described in Section

4.1. Some preliminary results are also given in that section. Section 4.2 gives the main theorems on L^{∞}-stability. The disturbance-free case is then considered in Section 4.3. The boundedness results are used to prove that part of the state vector, namely the output error $y-y^M$, converges to zero. This is a fairly satisfactory result for the deterministic case. Particularly, the convergence problems of the MRAS systems discussed in Chapter 2 are solved. Section 4.4 indicates some extensions of the stability analysis. Section 4.5 finally contains a discussion of the results.

4.1. Preliminaries

The algorithms described in Chapter 2 were divided into two broad cathegories, called *deterministic* or *stochastic* depending on the underlying design method. Expressed in another way, the two approaches deal with *fixed* or *estimated* observer polynomials. Results will be given for both types of algorithms but the details are worked out for the deterministic design case only.

For easy reference, some of the equations describing the algorithms will be given below.

Plant model

$$A(q^{-1})\ y(t) = b_0\ q^{-(k+1)}\ B(q^{-1})\ u(t) + w(t). \tag{4.1}$$

Here k is a nonnegative integer,

$$A(q^{-1}) = 1 + a_1\ q^{-1} + \ldots + a_n\ q^{-n}$$

$$B(q^{-1}) = 1 + b_1\ q^{-1} + \ldots + b_m\ q^{-m}$$

and w(t) is a disturbance which cannot be measured.

Reference model

$$y^M(t) = q^{-(k+1)}\ \frac{B^M(q^{-1})}{A^M(q^{-1})}\ u^M(t) = q^{-(k+1)}\ \frac{b_0^M + \ldots + b_m^M\ q^{-m}}{1 + a_1^M\ q^{-1} + \ldots\ a_n^M\ q^{-n}}\ u^M(t). \tag{4.2}$$

Here $A^M(q^{-1})$ is asymptotically stable and $u^M(t)$ is the command input.

Filtered error

$$e_f(t) = \frac{Q(q^{-1})}{P(q^{-1})} e(t) = \frac{Q(q^{-1})}{P_1(q^{-1})\, P_2(q^{-1})} [y(t) - y^M(t)], \tag{4.3}$$

where

$$Q(q^{-1}) = 1 + q_1 q^{-1} + \ldots + q_{n_Q} q^{-n_Q}$$

$$P_1(q^{-1}) = 1 + p_{11} q^{-1} + \ldots + p_{1n_{P_1}} q^{-n_{P_1}}$$

$$P_2(q^{-1}) = 1 + p_{21} q^{-1} + \ldots + p_{2n_{P_2}} q^{-n_{P_2}}$$

are all asymptotically stable polynomials.

Deterministic design

The observer polynomial

$$T(q^{-1}) = 1 + t_1 q^{-1} + \ldots + t_{n_T} q^{-n_T}$$

is chosen a priori. It is assumed that $T(q^{-1})$ is asymptotically stable. The estimation model is given by

$$e_f(t) = q^{-(k+1)}\left[b_0 \frac{\overline{u}(t)}{P_1} + b_0\, \theta^T \overline{\varphi}(t)\right] + \frac{QR}{TA^M P} w(t). \tag{4.4}$$

Here $\overline{x}$ denotes the signal obtained by filtering x with Q/TA^M and

$$\varphi^T(t) = \left[\frac{u(t-1)}{P}, \ldots, \frac{u(t-n_u)}{P}, \frac{y(t)}{P}, \ldots, \frac{y(t-n_y+1)}{P}, -\frac{TB^M}{P} u^M(t)\right], \tag{4.5}$$

where

$$n_u = \max\,(m+k,\ n_{P_2})$$

$$n_y = \max\,(n+n_T-k,\ n).$$

The description of the algorithms in Section 2.2 was quite general. There are many details where several choices can be made. For the analysis it is necessary to be more specific. Two prototype algorithms will be stated. They will be called the *DSA-algorithm* (Discrete time, Stochastic Approximation) and the *DLS-algorithm* (Discrete time, Least Squares) respectively. The deterministic versions are defined as follows.

DSA-ALGORITHM

- estimation:

$$\hat{b}_0(t) = \hat{b}_0(t-1) + \left(\frac{\bar{u}(t-k-1)}{P_1} + \hat{\theta}^T(t-1)\,\bar{\varphi}(t-k-1)\right)\frac{\varepsilon(t)}{r(t)} \tag{4.6a}$$

$$\hat{\theta}(t) = \hat{\theta}(t-1) + \beta_0\,\bar{\varphi}(t-k-1)\,\frac{\varepsilon(t)}{r(t)} \tag{4.6b}$$

$$r(t) = \lambda r(t-1) + \left(\frac{\bar{u}(t-k-1)}{P_1} + \hat{\theta}^T(t-1)\,\bar{\varphi}(t-k-1)\right)^2 + \beta_0^2\,|\bar{\varphi}(t-k-1)|^2 + \alpha; \quad 0 \leq \lambda < 1; \quad \alpha \geq 0 \tag{4.6c}$$

$$\varepsilon(t) = e_f(t) - \hat{e}_f(t|t-1) \tag{4.6d}$$

$$\hat{e}_f(t|t-1) = \hat{b}_0(t-1)\left[\frac{\bar{u}(t-k-1)}{P_1} + \hat{\theta}^T(t-1)\,\bar{\varphi}(t-k-1)\right] \tag{4.6e}$$

- control:

$$\frac{\bar{u}(t)}{P_1} = -\,\hat{\theta}^T(t)\,\bar{\varphi}(t). \tag{4.6f}$$

□

REMARK 1

The constant β_0 is an a priori estimate of b_0. The importance of the choice of β_0 for the stability properties will be discussed in Section 4.2.

□

REMARK 2

The stochastic approximation algorithm is a simple estimation scheme which has been used by several authors, e.g. Ionescu/Monopoli (1977) and Ljung (1977a). Note that λ is equal to one in a proper stochastic approximation scheme. This means that the "gain" in the algorithm is decreasing as 1/t when $t \to \infty$. This case is *not* covered in the analysis. Compare with the discussion in connection with Theorem 4.1 in the next section. The constant α may be included for numerical reasons. If $\alpha = 0$, it will be assumed that r(t) is made nonzero e.g. by using $\lambda > 0$ and a strictly positive initial value of r(t). Finally note that if $k = 0$ the estimation of b_0, (4.6a), is eliminated and also $\varepsilon(t) = e_f(t)$. This follows from (4.6f). □

REMARK 3

The control law (4.6f) is identical to the one discussed in Chapter 2, see (2.15). □

REMARK 4

Note that the filtering by the transfer function Q/TA^M is done as described in Section 2.4. This implies that no positive real condition is needed. More important is perhaps the fact that the filtering seems to improve the transient properties of the algorithms. This is illustrated in the following example. □

EXAMPLE 4.1

Consider a plant given by

$$(1 - 0.9\ q^{-1})\ y(t) = u(t-1).$$

Let the reference model be

$$(1 - 0.7\ q^{-1})\ y^M(t) = 0.3\ u^M(t-1).$$

The plant is controlled by the MRAS by Ionescu and Monopoli. It is seen in Example 2.1 that the polynomials should be chosen as

$$Q = P = T = 1$$

and the transfer function $P_2/A^M = 1\,/\,(1 - 0.7\ q^{-1})$ is then strictly positive real. The estimation scheme in the DSA-algorithm is used with $\beta_0 = 1$, $\alpha = 0$, and $\lambda = 0.2$. Two parameters have to be estimated, namely $s_0 = 0.2$ and $1/b_0 = 1$. The behaviour of the algorithm is shown in Figures 4.1 - 4.3 when u^M is a square wave. The original algorithm has an oscillatory transient behaviour as seen in Fig. 4.1. These oscillations are eliminated if the signals are filtered by Q/TA^M as in the DSA-algorithm. This can be seen in Fig. 4.2. It should be noted that the effects can be more or less pronounced with different choices of λ. Similar observations have been made in many cases. In Fig. 4.3 it is shown that the oscillations can be reduced with a different λ but the parameter convergence is still much slower than if the filtering is used. □

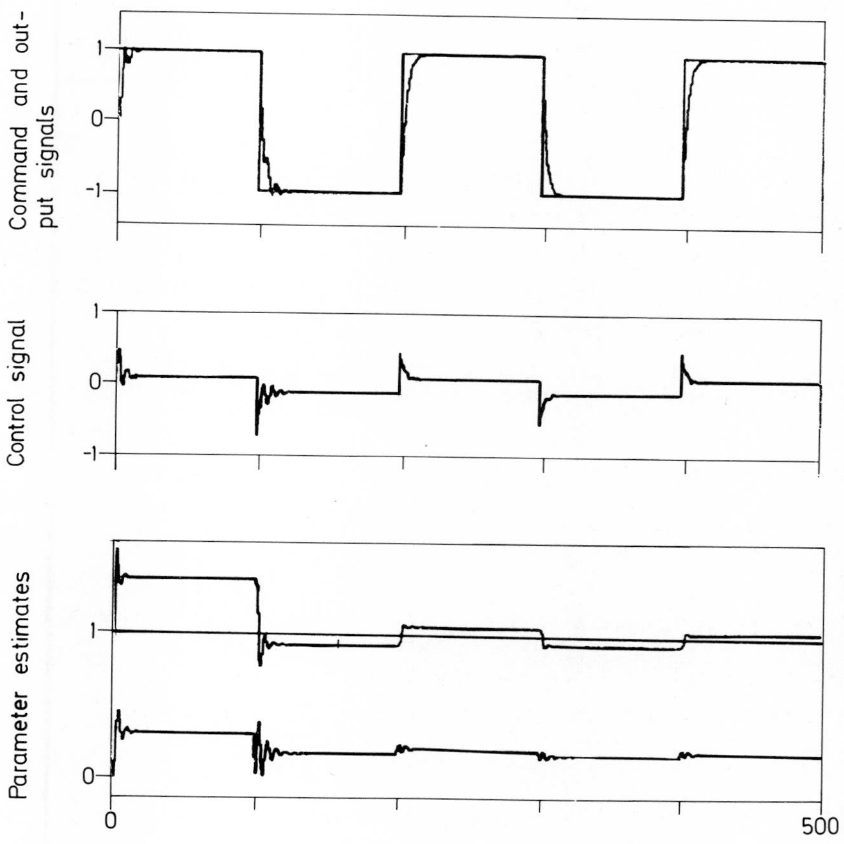

Figure 4.1. Command, output, and control signals and parameter estimates for Example 4.1 without filtering by Q/TA^M.

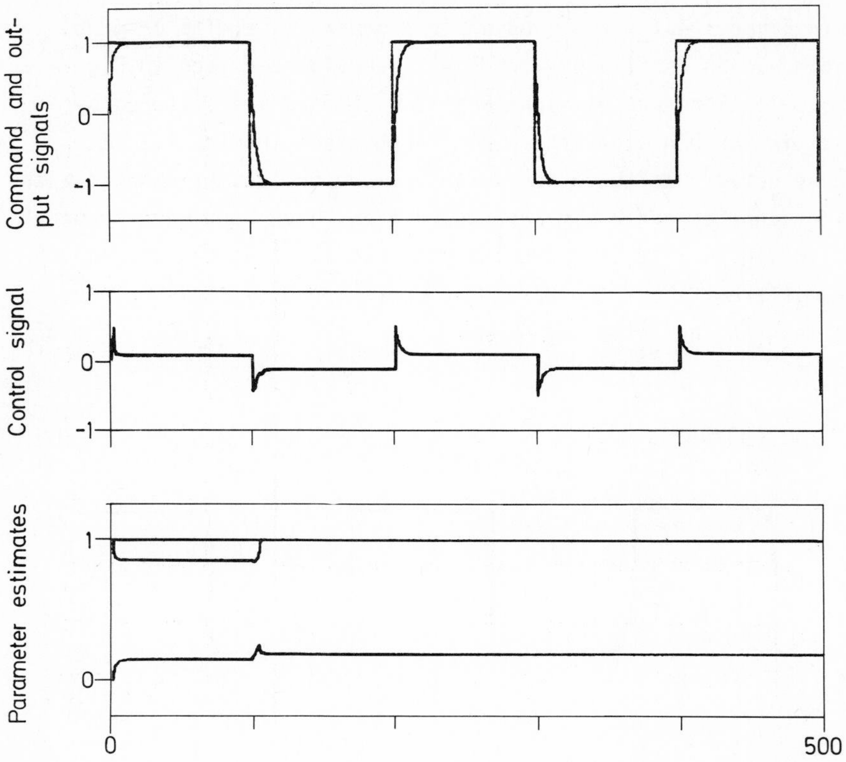

Figure 4.2. Command, output, and control signals and parameter estimates for Example 4.1 with filtering by Q/TA^M.

The DLS-algorithm is defined analogously to the DSA-algorithm. Since the stability proof requires that b_0 is known, the algorithm is stated for this case only. Some changes are then needed. Firstly, the estimation of b_0 as in (4.6a) is eliminated. Secondly, the vector θ was previously defined to have $1/b_0$ as its last element. Since b_0 is assumed known, it is now not included in θ. With obvious notation the estimation model (4.4) is replaced by

$$y_f(t) = q^{-(k+1)} \left[b_0 \frac{\overline{u}(t)}{P_1} + b_0 \, \theta^T \overline{\varphi}(t) \right] + \frac{QR}{TA^M P} w(t), \tag{4.7}$$

where $\varphi(t)$ does not contain the last component in (4.5). The DLS-algorithm is defined as follows.

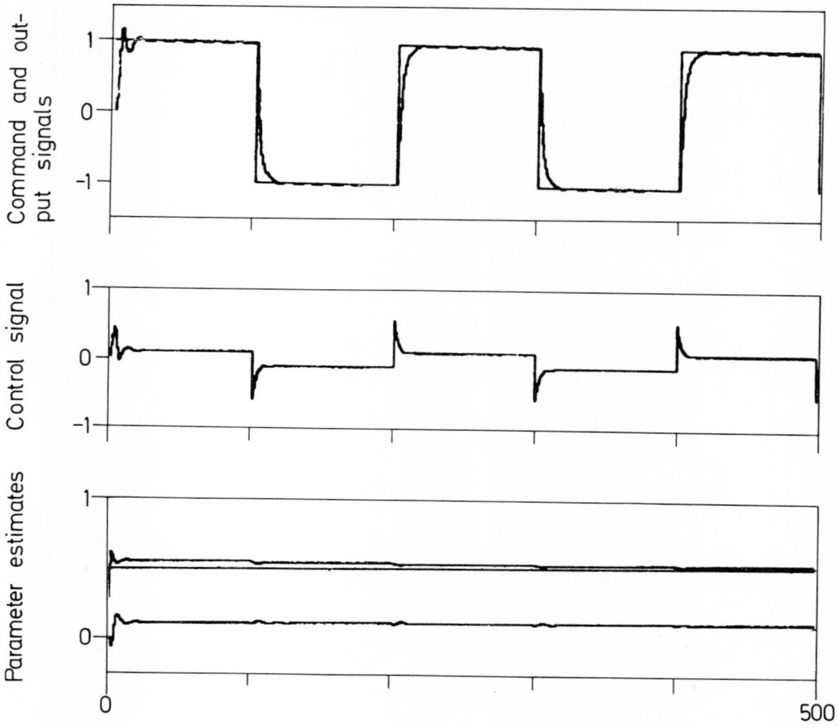

Figure 4.3. Command, output, and control signals and parameter estimates for Example 4.1 without filtering by Q/TA^M and with $\lambda = 0.8$.

DLS-ALGORITHM (b_0 *known*)

- estimation:

$$\begin{cases} \hat{\theta}(t) = \hat{\theta}(t-1) + \frac{1}{b_0} P(t)\, \overline{\varphi}(t-k-1)\, \varepsilon(t) & (4.8a) \\ P^{-1}(t) = \lambda P^{-1}(t-1) + \overline{\varphi}(t-k-1)\, \overline{\varphi}^T(t-k-1); \quad 0 \leq \lambda < 1 & (4.8b) \\ \varepsilon(t) = y_f(t) - \hat{y}_f(t|t-1) & (4.8c) \\ \hat{y}_f(t|t-1) = b_0\left[\frac{\overline{u}(t-k-1)}{P_1} + \hat{\theta}^T(t-1)\, \overline{\varphi}(t-k-1)\right] & (4.8d) \end{cases}$$

- control:

$$\frac{\overline{u}(t)}{P_1} = -\hat{\theta}^T(t)\, \overline{\varphi}(t) + \frac{1}{b_0} \frac{QB^M}{PA^M} u^M(t) \qquad (4.8e)$$

□

REMARK

The updating of the matrix $P^{-1}(t)$, (4.7b), is in practise replaced by an equivalent updating of its inverse P(t):

$$P(t) = \frac{1}{\lambda}\left[P(t-1) - \frac{P(t-1)\,\overline{\varphi}(t-k-1)\,\overline{\varphi}^T(t-k-1)\,P(t-1)}{\lambda + \overline{\varphi}^T(t-k-1)\,P(t-1)\,\overline{\varphi}(t-k-1)}\right]. \tag{4.8f}$$

□

Stochastic design

It was seen in Section 2.2 that a model similar to (4.4) can be obtained in the stochastic design case where $w(t) = C(q^{-1})\,v(t)$. The parameter vector θ is then augmented with the unknown C-parameters divided by b_0 and the vector $\varphi(t)$ is redefined as

$$\varphi^T(t) = \left[\frac{u(t-1)}{P}, \ldots, \frac{u(t-n_u)}{P}, \frac{y(t)}{P}, \ldots, \frac{y(t-n_y+1)}{P},\right.$$
$$\left. -\frac{B^M}{P}\,u^M(t), \ldots, -\frac{B^M}{P}\,u^M(t-n)\right]. \tag{4.9}$$

The model corresponding to (4.4) is then

$$e_f(t) = q^{-(k+1)}\,\frac{1}{C}\left[b_0\,\frac{\overline{u}(t)}{P_1} + b_0\,\theta^T\,\overline{\varphi}(t)\right] + \frac{QR}{CA^MP}\,w(t), \tag{4.10}$$

where '$\overline{}$' now denotes filtering by Q/A^M. Note that it is not possible to filter by 1/C since C is unknown. The prediction $\hat{e}_f(t|t-1)$ is calculated as described in Section 2.2:

$$\hat{e}_f(t|t-1) = \hat{b}_0(t-1)\left[\frac{\overline{u}(t-k-1)}{P_1} + \hat{\theta}^T(t-1)\,\overline{\varphi}(t-k-1)\right]. \tag{4.11}$$

The definitions of the DSA- and the DLS-algorithms are still valid with these new interpretations of θ, φ, and '$\overline{}$'. The equations are identical and are therefore not repeated.

It is convenient for the stability proofs to have a representation like (4.10) but without the unknown C-polynomial. Note that (4.10) was obtained using the identity

$$CA^M = AR + q^{-(k+1)}\,S,$$

where the degree of R was k and the degree of S was $\max(n+n_T-k-1,\ n-1)$. Use instead the identity

$$A^M = AR_0 + q^{-(k+1)}\,S_0.$$

If degree $(R_0) = k$, then the degree of S_0 will be at most n-1, i.e. less than or equal to the degree of S. Using this identity, another representation like (4.10) is obtained with *the same φ-vector* but a different θ-vector, here called θ_0:

$$e_f(t) = q^{-(k+1)}\left[b_0\,\frac{\overline{u}(t)}{P_1} + b_0\,\theta_0^T\,\overline{\varphi}(t)\right] + \frac{QR_0}{A^M P}\,w(t). \tag{4.12}$$

Here '‾' still denotes filtering by Q/A^M. This representation is convenient because the prediction $\hat{e}_f(t|t-1)$ is calculated without the C-polynomial, see (4.11).

General assumptions

The following general assumptions are made:

A1) The number of plant poles n and zeros m are known.

A2) The time delay k is known and the sign of the nonzero constant b_0 is known. Without loss of generality b_0 will be assumed positive.

A3) The plant is minimum phase.

These assumptions were all introduced and discussed in Chapter 2.

Basic lemmas

Some basic lemmas, which will be used several times in the proofs, are given below. The first lemma relates the evolution of $\varphi(t)$ to the command input u^M, the disturbance w and to the error $e = y - y^M$.

LEMMA 4.1

Consider the plant (4.1). Assume that it is minimum phase. Then $\varphi(t)$, defined by (4.5) or (4.9), satisfies

$$\varphi(t+1) = F\,\varphi(t) + \begin{pmatrix} \frac{1}{b_0}\cdot\frac{A}{P}\, e(t+k+1) \\ 0 \\ \vdots \\ 0 \\ \frac{1}{P}\, e(t+1) \\ 0 \\ \vdots \\ 0 \end{pmatrix} + \begin{pmatrix} -\frac{1}{b_0}\cdot\frac{1}{P}\, w(t+k+1) \\ 0 \\ \vdots \\ \vdots \\ 0 \end{pmatrix} + U^M(t+1) \tag{4.13}$$

where the constant matrix F has all its eigenvalues inside the unit disc and U^M is a vector whose components are outputs of asymptotically stable filters with u^M as the input. □

Proof

The proof is given for the deterministic design only. The proof for the stochastic design is, however, almost identical. From (4.5) and (4.1) it follows that

$$\varphi(t+1) = \begin{pmatrix} \frac{u(t)}{P} \\ \vdots \\ \frac{u(t-n_u+1)}{P} \\ \frac{y(t+1)}{P} \\ \vdots \\ \frac{y(t-n_y+2)}{P} \\ -\frac{TB^M}{P}u^M(t+1) \end{pmatrix} = \left(\begin{array}{cccc|cccc|c} -b_1 & \cdots & -b_m & 0\ldots 0 & & & & & \\ 1 & & & & & & & & \\ & \ddots & & & & & & & \\ & & 1 & 0 & & & & & \\ \hline & & & & 0 & & & & \\ & & & & 1 & & & & \\ & & & & & \ddots & & & \\ & & & & & & 1 & 0 & \\ \hline & & & & & & & & 0 \end{array}\right) \varphi(t) +$$

$$
+ \begin{pmatrix} \frac{1}{b_0 P}\left[Ay(t+k+1) - w(t+k+1)\right] \\ 0 \\ \vdots \\ 0 \\ \frac{y(t+1)}{P} \\ 0 \\ \vdots \\ 0 \\ -\frac{TB^M}{P}u^M(t+1) \end{pmatrix} \triangleq F\,\varphi(t) + g(t),
$$

where F is asymptotically stable because the plant is minimum phase. Note that the fact that $m \leqslant n_u$ has been used. From (4.3),

$$
y(t) = e(t) + y^M(t) = e(t) + q^{-(k+1)}\frac{B^M}{A^M}u^M(t)
$$

which implies that

$$
g(t) = \begin{pmatrix} \frac{1}{b_0 P}\left[Ay(t+k+1) - w(t+k+1)\right] \\ 0 \\ \vdots \\ 0 \\ \frac{y(t+1)}{P} \\ 0 \\ \vdots \\ 0 \\ -\frac{TB^M}{P}u^M(t+1) \end{pmatrix} =
$$

$$
= \begin{pmatrix} \frac{1}{b_0} \cdot \frac{A}{P} e(t+k+1) \\ 0 \\ \vdots \\ 0 \\ \frac{e(t+1)}{P} \\ 0 \\ \vdots \\ 0 \end{pmatrix} + \begin{pmatrix} -\frac{1}{b_0} \cdot \frac{w(t+k+1)}{P} \\ 0 \\ \vdots \\ \vdots \\ 0 \end{pmatrix} + \begin{pmatrix} \frac{AB^M}{b_0 PA^M} u^M(t) \\ 0 \\ \vdots \\ 0 \\ \frac{B^M}{PA^M} u^M(t-k) \\ 0 \\ \vdots \\ 0 \\ -\frac{TB^M}{P} u^M(t+1) \end{pmatrix}
$$

This is equivalent to (4.13). □

Define

$$
\begin{aligned}
\tilde{b}_0(t) &= \hat{b}_0(t) - b_0 \\
\tilde{\theta}(t) &= \begin{cases} \hat{\theta}(t) - \theta & \text{in the deterministic design case,} \\ \hat{\theta}(t) - \theta_0 & \text{in the stochastic design case.} \end{cases}
\end{aligned} \tag{4.14}
$$

LEMMA 4.2

Let $\tilde{b}_0(t)$ and $\tilde{\theta}(t)$ be defined by (4.14). Assume that $0 < \frac{b_0}{2} < \beta_0$. Then the following holds for the DSA-algorithm for deterministic design, (4.6):

$$
\tilde{b}_0^2(t) + \frac{b_0}{\beta_0} |\tilde{\theta}(t)|^2 \leq \tilde{b}_0^2(t-1) + \frac{b_0}{\beta_0} |\tilde{\theta}(t-1)|^2 - c\,\frac{\varepsilon^2(t)}{r(t)} +
$$

$$
+ \frac{1}{cr(t)} \left(\frac{R}{P}\,\overline{w}(t)\right)^2 \qquad \forall\ t \geq k+1, \tag{4.15}
$$

where c is a positive constant. □

Proof

Write (4.6 a,b) in terms of $\tilde{b}_0(t)$ and $\tilde{\theta}(t)$ and multiply them by their transposes:

$$\tilde{b}_0^2(t) = \tilde{b}_0^2(t-1) + 2\tilde{b}_0(t-1)\,\frac{\varepsilon(t)}{r(t)}\left(\frac{\overline{u}(t-k-1)}{P_1} + \hat{\theta}^T(t-1)\,\overline{\varphi}(t-k-1)\right) +$$

$$+ \frac{\varepsilon^2(t)}{r^2(t)}\left(\frac{\overline{u}(t-k-1)}{P_1} + \hat{\theta}^T(t-1)\,\overline{\varphi}(t-k-1)\right)^2$$

$$|\tilde{\theta}(t)|^2 = |\tilde{\theta}(t-1)|^2 + \frac{2\beta_0\varepsilon(t)}{r(t)}\,\tilde{\theta}^T(t-1)\,\overline{\varphi}(t-k-1) +$$

$$+ \beta_0^2\,\frac{\varepsilon^2(t)}{r^2(t)}\,|\overline{\varphi}(t-k-1)|^2.$$

Add the second equation, multiplied by $\frac{b_0}{\beta_0}$, to the first equation, which gives

$$\tilde{b}_0^2(t) + \frac{b_0}{\beta_0}|\tilde{\theta}(t)|^2 - \left(\tilde{b}_0^2(t-1) + \frac{b_0}{\beta_0}|\tilde{\theta}(t-1)|^2\right) =$$

$$= \frac{2\varepsilon(t)}{r(t)}\left[\tilde{b}_0(t-1)\left(\frac{\overline{u}(t-k-1)}{P_1} + \hat{\theta}^T(t-1)\overline{\varphi}(t-k-1)\right) + b_0\,\tilde{\theta}^T(t-1)\overline{\varphi}(t-k-1)\right] +$$

$$+ \frac{\varepsilon^2(t)}{r^2(t)}\left[\left(\frac{\overline{u}(t-k-1)}{P_1} + \hat{\theta}^T(t-1)\overline{\varphi}(t-k-1)\right)^2 + b_0\,\beta_0\,|\overline{\varphi}(t-k-1)|^2\right] \leq$$

$$\leq \frac{2\varepsilon(t)}{r(t)}\left(\frac{R}{P}\,\overline{w}(t) - \varepsilon(t)\right) +$$

$$+ \max\left(1, \frac{b_0}{\beta_0}\right)\frac{\varepsilon^2(t)}{r^2(t)}\left[\left(\frac{\overline{u}(t-k-1)}{P_1} + \hat{\theta}^T(t-1)\overline{\varphi}(t-k-1)\right)^2 + \beta_0^2\,|\overline{\varphi}(t-k-1)|^2\right],$$

where (4.4), (4.6e) and (4.14) are used in the last step. Let

$$c = 1 - \frac{1}{2}\max\left(1, \frac{b_0}{\beta_0}\right).$$

Then c is positive from the assumptions. Insert this into the inequality above and use (4.6c) to obtain

$$\tilde{b}_0^2(t) + \frac{b_0}{\beta_0}|\tilde{\theta}(t)|^2 - \left(\tilde{b}_0^2(t-1) + \frac{b_0}{\beta_0}|\tilde{\theta}(t-1)|^2\right) \leq$$

$$\leq \frac{2\varepsilon(t)}{r(t)} \left(\frac{R}{P}\, \overline{w}(t) - \varepsilon(t)\right) + 2(1-c)\, \frac{\varepsilon^2(t)}{r(t)} =$$

$$= \frac{1}{r(t)} \left[- \left(\sqrt{c}\; \varepsilon(t) - \frac{1}{\sqrt{c}}\; \frac{R}{P}\, \overline{w}(t)\right)^2 - c\,\varepsilon^2(t) + \frac{1}{c} \left(\frac{R}{P}\, \overline{w}(t)\right)^2\right] \leq$$

$$\leq - c\, \frac{\varepsilon^2(t)}{r(t)} + \frac{1}{cr(t)} \left(\frac{R}{P}\, \overline{w}(t)\right)^2,$$

which concludes the proof. □

Corollary

The same result holds for the DSA-algorithm with stochastic design if R is replaced by R_0 and $\varphi(t)$ is defined by (4.9). □

Proof

The same proof still holds. □

A corresponding result concerning the DLS-algorithm with known b_0 is given in the following lemma.

LEMMA 4.3

Let $\tilde{\theta}(t)$ be defined by (4.14). Assume that b_0 is known. Then the following holds for the DLS-algorithm for the deterministic design, (4.8):

$$\tilde{\theta}^T(t)\; P^{-1}(t)\; \tilde{\theta}(t) = \lambda\; \tilde{\theta}^T(t-1)\; P^{-1}(t-1)\; \tilde{\theta}(t-1) -$$

$$- \frac{\lambda}{\lambda + \overline{\varphi}^T(t-k-1)\, P(t-1)\, \overline{\varphi}(t-k-1)}\; \frac{\varepsilon^2(t)}{b_0^2} + \frac{1}{b_0^2} \left(\frac{R(q^{-1})}{P(q^{-1})}\, \overline{w}(t)\right)^2. \qquad (4.16)$$

□

Proof

Write (4.8a) in terms of $\tilde{\theta}(t)$ and multiply from the left by $P^{-1/2}(t)$. This gives

$$P^{-1/2}(t)\; \tilde{\theta}(t) = P^{-1/2}(t)\; \tilde{\theta}(t-1) + \frac{1}{b_0}\, P^{1/2}(t)\; \overline{\varphi}(t-k-1)\; \varepsilon(t)$$

and after multiplication with the transpose

$$\tilde{\theta}^T(t)\ P^{-1}(t)\ \tilde{\theta}(t) = \tilde{\theta}^T(t-1)\ P^{-1}(t)\ \tilde{\theta}(t-1)\ +$$

$$+ \frac{2}{b_0}\ \tilde{\theta}^T(t-1)\,\overline{\varphi}(t-k-1)\,\varepsilon(t) + \frac{1}{b_0^2}\,\overline{\varphi}^T(t-k-1)\,P(t)\,\overline{\varphi}(t-k-1)\ \varepsilon^2(t) =$$

$$= \lambda\ \tilde{\theta}^T(t-1)\ P^{-1}(t-1)\ \tilde{\theta}(t-1) + [\tilde{\theta}^T(t-1)\ \overline{\varphi}(t-k-1)]^2 +$$

$$+ \frac{2}{b_0}\ \tilde{\theta}^T(t-1)\ \overline{\varphi}(t-k-1)\ \varepsilon(t) + \frac{1}{b_0^2}\ \overline{\varphi}^T(t-k-1)\ P(t)\ \overline{\varphi}(t-k-1)\ \varepsilon^2(t).$$

If (4.7), (4.8d) and (4.14) are used, the following is obtained:

$$\tilde{\theta}^T(t)\ P^{-1}(t)\ \tilde{\theta}(t) - \lambda\ \tilde{\theta}^T(t-1)\ P^{-1}(t-1)\ \tilde{\theta}(t-1) =$$

$$= \frac{1}{b_0^2}\left(\frac{R}{P}\,\overline{w}(t) - \varepsilon(t)\right)^2 + \frac{2}{b_0^2}\left(\frac{R}{P}\,\overline{w}(t) - \varepsilon(t)\right)\varepsilon(t) +$$

$$+ \frac{1}{b_0^2}\ \overline{\varphi}^T(t-k-1)\ P(t)\ \overline{\varphi}(t-k-1)\ \varepsilon^2(t). \qquad (4.17)$$

The updating formula for P(t) is given by (4.8f). Multiply this equation from the left by $\overline{\varphi}^T(t-k-1)$ and from the right by $\overline{\varphi}(t-k-1)$. This gives

$$\overline{\varphi}^T(t-k-1)\ P(t)\ \overline{\varphi}(t-k-1) = \frac{\overline{\varphi}^T(t-k-1)\ P(t-1)\ \overline{\varphi}(t-k-1)}{\lambda + \overline{\varphi}^T(t-k-1)\ P(t-1)\ \overline{\varphi}(t-k-1)}\ .$$

Insert this into the equation (4.17) to get:

$$\tilde{\theta}^T(t)\ P^{-1}(t)\ \tilde{\theta}(t) - \lambda\ \tilde{\theta}^T(t-1)\ P^{-1}(t-1)\ \tilde{\theta}(t-1) =$$

$$= -\frac{\varepsilon^2(t)}{b_0^2} + \frac{1}{b_0^2}\left(\frac{R}{P}\,\overline{w}(t)\right)^2 + \frac{1}{b_0^2}\ \frac{\overline{\varphi}^T(t-k-1)\ P(t-1)\ \overline{\varphi}(t-k-1)}{\lambda + \overline{\varphi}^T(t-k-1)\,P(t-1)\,\overline{\varphi}(t-k-1)}\ \varepsilon^2(t) =$$

$$= -\frac{\lambda}{\lambda + \overline{\varphi}^T(t-k-1)\ P(t-1)\ \overline{\varphi}(t-k-1)}\ \frac{\varepsilon^2(t)}{b_0^2} + \frac{1}{b_0^2}\left(\frac{R}{P}\,\overline{w}(t)\right)^2,$$

which is identical to (4.16). □

Corollary

The same result holds for the DLS-algorithm with stochastic design if R is replaced by R_0 and $\varphi(t)$ is defined by (4.9). □

Proof

The proof remains the same. □

The results of Lemma 4.2 and Lemma 4.3 can be interpreted in the following way. The estimation errors $\tilde{b}_0$ and $\tilde{\theta}$ decrease if the prediction error $\varepsilon(t)$ is large. On the other hand, the errors increase if the noise magnitude is large. This is natural intuitively.

4.2. L^∞-stability

The main results on L^∞-stability will be given in this section. For convenience, make the following

DEFINITION

The closed loop system is L^∞-*stable* if uniformly bounded disturbance (w) and command (u^M) signals give uniformly bounded input (u) and output (y) signals. □

It will thus be assumed in the sequel that w(t) and $u^M(t)$ are uniformly bounded.

The main part of this section is devoted to the DSA-algorithm. The idea behind the stability analysis is the heuristic argument given in the beginning of this chapter. It was pointed out that there are some shortcomings of the argument. Firstly, it is necessary to show that not only a few of the parameter estimates become accurate when the signals are growing large. This is no problem for the DSA-algorithm. The second problem mentioned seems to be more difficult. It takes some time for the estimates to become accurate even if the signals are very large. The discussion thus requires that the output does not increase arbitrarily fast and that the parameter adjustment is not too slow. The latter condition is the reason why we do not consider estimation algorithms with decreasing gains. Compare the definitions of the DSA- and DLS-algorithms. The possibility that the output may increase arbitrarily fast is closely related to the magnitude of the parameter estimates. It will be eliminated by guaranteeing that the estimates are bounded. The following example illustrates that unbounded parameter estimates can lead to instability.

EXAMPLE 4.2

Consider a plant given by

$$y(t) + a\, y(t-1) = b_0\, u(t-1) + w(t),$$

where b_0 is known to be unity. Assume that the reference model is

$$y^M(t) = u^M(t-1).$$

Choose Q = P = T = 1. Equation (4.4) can then be written as

$$y(t) - y^M(t) = u(t-1) + s\, y(t-1) - u^M(t-1) + w(t), \tag{4.18}$$

where s = -a. Since b_0 is known, the prediction error can be written as

$$\varepsilon(t) = - \tilde{s}(t-1)\, y(t-1) + w(t), \tag{4.19}$$

where

$$\tilde{s}(t) = \hat{s}(t) - s.$$

With $\lambda = 0$ and $\alpha = 1$ in the DSA-algorithm the updating of the parameter estimate is given by

$$\hat{s}(t) = \hat{s}(t-1) + y(t-1)\, \frac{\varepsilon(t)}{1 + y^2(t-1)} .$$

This equation can be expressed in $\tilde{s}(t)$ as

$$\tilde{s}(t) = \tilde{s}(t-1) + y(t-1)\, \frac{w(t) - \tilde{s}(t-1)\, y(t-1)}{1 + y^2(t-1)} . \tag{4.20}$$

The control law corresponding to (4.6f) is

$$u(t) = - \hat{s}(t)\, y(t) + u^M(t),$$

which can be inserted into (4.18) to give

$$y(t) = - \tilde{s}(t-1)\, y(t-1) + u^M(t-1) + w(t). \tag{4.21}$$

Eqs. (4.20) and (4.21) describe the closed loop system.

The basic idea with the example is to show that the closed loop system is unstable by finding a disturbance w and a command input u^M such that the parameter error $\tilde{s}(t)$ can increase without limit. Thus, assume that the recursion (4.20), (4.21) starts at $t=1$ with $\tilde{s}(1) = 0$, $y(1) = 1$. Define

$$f(t) \triangleq \left(\sqrt{t(t-1)} - (t-1)\right)\left(1 + \frac{1}{t-1}\right), \qquad t = 2, 3, \ldots, T-5,$$

for some large T. Choose the following disturbance

$$w(t) = 1 - \frac{1}{\sqrt{t-1}} + f(t), \qquad t = 2, 3, \ldots, T-5,$$

and the following command signal

$$u^M(t-1) = \frac{1}{\sqrt{t}} - f(t), \qquad t = 2, 3, \ldots, T-5.$$

The signals w and u^M are bounded. It is then easy to show that

$$\tilde{s}(t) = \sqrt{t} - 1$$

$$y(t) = \frac{1}{\sqrt{t}}$$

for $t = 1, \ldots, T-5$. Further, let

$$w(t) = 0, \; t = T-4, \ldots, T$$

$$u^M(t-1) = \begin{cases} 0, & t = T-4 \\ 1, & t = T-3, \ldots, T. \end{cases}$$

It is then easy to check that $\tilde{s}(t)$ and $y(t)$ for large T are approximately given by:

t	$\tilde{s}(t)$	$y(t)$
T - 4	$\sqrt{T}$	-1
T - 3	$\frac{\sqrt{T}}{2}$	$\sqrt{T}$
T - 2	$\frac{1}{2\sqrt{T}}$	$-\frac{T}{2}$
T - 1	$\frac{1}{\sqrt{T}T^2}$	$\frac{\sqrt{T}}{4}$
T	$\frac{16}{\sqrt{T}T^3}$	1

Now choose $w(T+1)$ and $u^M(T)$ such that $\tilde{s}(T+1) = 0$ and $y(T+1) = 1$. The state vector of (4.20), (4.21) is then equal to the initial state. By repeating the procedure for increasing values of T, a subsequence of $y(t)$ will increase as $-\frac{T}{2}$ and therefore is unbounded. The result of a simulation with $T = 50, 100, 150, \ldots$ is shown in Fig. 4.4. □

The example shows that bounded disturbance and command signals can be found such that the output is unbounded. The assumption of bounded

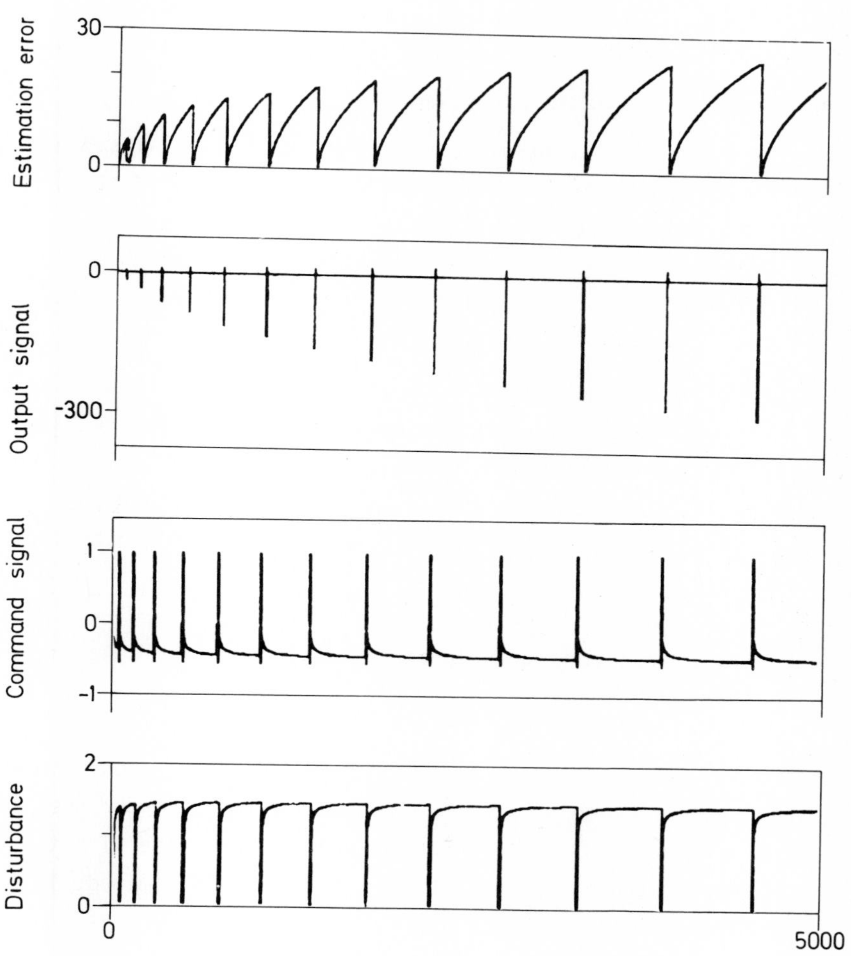

Figure 4.4. Simulation results for Example 4.2.

disturbance and command signals is thus not sufficient to guarantee L^∞-stability. Some additional assumption is needed. Boundedness of parameter estimates is chosen here and other possibilities are discussed in Section 4.5. It should finally be noted that the same technique can be used to derive examples of instability with any $\lambda < 1$.

L^∞-stability for the DSA-algorithm

The main result on L^∞-stability for the DSA-algorithm is given in the following theorem.

THEOREM 4.1 (DSA-algorithm with noise)

Consider the plant (4.1) controlled by the DSA-algorithm with deterministic or stochastic design. Assume that assumptions A1 - A3 are satisfied. Moreover assume that the parameter estimates are uniformly bounded and that $b_0 < 2\beta_0$. Then the closed-loop system is L^∞-stable.

□

Proof

The full proof for the deterministic design is given in Appendix A. It can be concluded immediately that the proof holds also for the stochastic design, using the representation (4.12) instead of (4.10). Some minor changes are needed, such as replacing R by R_0 and Q/TA^M by Q/A^M. The φ-vector will also contain more u^M-components in the stochastic design case, see (4.9).

The proof of the theorem is unfortunately fairly technical. An outline of the proof will therefore be given.

The idea of the proof is to examine the behaviour of the algorithm when $|\overline{\varphi}(t)|$ is growing from an arbitrarily large value to a larger one. The time interval under consideration can be shown to increase with the difference between the values if the rate of growth is limited. This is done in Step 1 of the proof.

It follows from Lemma 4.1 that e(t) must be large when $|\overline{\varphi}(t)|$ increases.

It must in fact be of the order of $|\overline{\varphi}(t)|$ many times if the interval where $|\overline{\varphi}(t)|$ increases is long. This is shown in the first part of Step 3 of the proof. Since r(t) is of the order of $|\overline{\varphi}(t)|^2$ and $\varepsilon(t)$ is of the order of e(t), it then follows from Lemma 4.2 that the parameter errors decrease significantly at many time instants. Neglecting the noise term, it thus follows from the boundedness of the estimates that there is a contradiction, which implies that arbitrarily large values of $|\overline{\varphi}(t)|$ do not exist. This is shown in the second part of Step 3. However, if the disturbance w(t) is nonzero the parameter errors could increase in the intervals between any two time instants where they decrease. See Lemma 4.2. Hence, it is important to get an upper bound on the length of these intervals. This is done in Step 2 of the proof, which utilizes the same kind of arguments as Step 3. □

The conditions of the theorem have all been discussed earlier, except for the condition $b_0 < 2\beta_0$. This condition enters via Lemma 4.2. It will be shown below that the condition is in fact necessary for global stability. Consider, however, first the local stability properties. For simplicity assume that $k = 0$ and that $w = 0$. Linearize the equations for the closed-loop system around the true parameter values and a constant u^M. It is then straightforward to verify that the eigenvalues corresponding to Eq. (4.6b) are all but one equal to one and one eigenvalue is equal to $1 - b_0(1-\lambda)/\beta_0$. A necessary condition for local stability is thus that $\beta_0 > b_0(1-\lambda)/2$. It is interesting to note that the condition requires only that β_0 is positive in the limit case $\lambda = 1$. This is exactly the condition which is met in the convergence analysis in presense of noise in Ljung/Wittenmark (1974).

It will be shown in the following example that the condition $\beta_0 > b_0(1-\lambda)/2$ must be strengthened to $\beta_0 > b_0/2$ in order to assure *global* stability. The condition is also discussed in Åström/Wittenmark (1973) and Ljung/Wittenmark (1974).

EXAMPLE 4.3

Consider the plant and the controller described in Example 4.1. If u^M

is set to zero, only one parameter is estimated, namely s_0. It is easy to check that the estimation error $\tilde{s}_0(t)$ is given by

$$\tilde{s}_0(t) = \tilde{s}_0(t-1)\left(1 - \beta_0 \frac{y^2(t-1)}{\lambda r(t-1) + \beta_0^2\, y^2(t-1)}\right).$$

Let $r(0) = 0$ and $y(0) = 1$. Assume that $\beta_0 = \frac{1}{2} - \delta$ for some arbitrarily small $\delta > 0$. Straightforward calculations then show that $|y(t)|$ tends to infinity if

$$\tilde{s}_0(0) > \max\left(1, \frac{\lambda\beta_0}{(1-\lambda)\,\delta}\right).$$

The closed-loop system is thus not globally stable with this choice of β_0. □

Several results on boundedness of the closed-loop signals can be derived from Theorem 4.1. Consider first the case where the disturbance w(t) is zero. This is the situation most often analysed in connection with model reference adaptive regulators. The following theorem gives a solution to the boundedness problem discussed before.

THEOREM 4.2 (DSA-algorithm without noise)

Consider the plant (4.1) with no noise, i.e. $w(t) = 0$, controlled by the DSA-algorithm with deterministic design, (4.6). Assume that A1 - A3 are fulfilled and that $b_0 < 2\beta_0$. Then the closed-loop system is L^∞-stable. □

Proof

It follows from Lemma 4.2 that the parameter estimates are bounded if $w(t) = 0$. Theorem 4.1 then gives the result. □

The corresponding result is also true for the stochastic design case. The result is however not given, because it seems unrealistic to assume that there is no noise when the decision has been made to estimate the optimal observer from noise characteristics.

It appears that the conditions for the stability result above are fairly mild. The condition on β_0 has been shown to be necessary for global stability. Also, the choice $\lambda < 1$ is the common one in real applications. However, the assumption that the disturbance is equal to zero is not very satisfactory. It would thus be desirable to improve the result in Theorem 4.1 without the a priori assumption of boundedness of parameter estimates. Below are presented two stability results, which treat modified versions of the DSA-algorithm.

THEOREM 4.3 (DSA-algorithm with conditional updating)

Consider the plant (4.1), controlled by the DSA-algorithm with deterministic or stochastic design, modified in the following way:

$$\left.\begin{aligned}\hat{b}_0(t) &= \hat{b}_0(t-1)\\ \hat{\theta}(t) &= \hat{\theta}(t-1)\end{aligned}\right\} \quad \text{if} \quad |\varepsilon(t)| < \frac{2\,K_w}{2-\max\,(b_0/\beta_0,\ 1)}, \tag{4.22}$$

where

$$\sup_t \left| \frac{R}{P}\,\overline{w}(t) \right| \leq K_w. \tag{4.23}$$

Assume that A1 - A3 are fulfilled and that $b_0 < 2\beta_0$. Then the closed-loop system is L^∞-stable.

Proof

As before, the proof is given for the deterministic design only. Lemma 4.2 gives together with (4.23)

$$\tilde{b}_0^2(t) + \frac{b_0}{\beta_0}\,|\tilde{\theta}(t)|^2 - \left(\tilde{b}_0^2(t-1) + \frac{b_0}{\beta_0}\,|\tilde{\theta}(t)|^2\right) \leq$$

$$\leq -\,c\,\frac{\varepsilon^2(t)}{r(t)} + \frac{1}{cr(t)}\left(\frac{R}{P}\,\overline{w}(t)\right)^2 = -\,\frac{c}{r(t)}\left[\varepsilon^2(t) - \left(\frac{\frac{R}{P}\,\overline{w}(t)}{c}\right)^2\right] \leq 0$$

if

$$|\varepsilon(t)| \geq \frac{K_w}{c} \geq \frac{2}{2-\max\,(b_0/\beta_0,\ 1)} \cdot \sup_t \left(\frac{R}{P}\,\overline{w}(t)\right).$$

Combined with (4.22) this implies that the parameter estimates are bounded. However, this does not imply that Theorem 4.1 can be applied straightforwardly, because the algorithm has been modified. Some changes are needed because Lemma 4.2 is no longer true at all times. The following minor changes of the proof in Appendix A have to be made:

(i) Lemma 4.2 is exploited in Step 2 of the proof, when (A.28) is derived. Note that the lemma is not necessarily valid for all times in the interval $[T^i_{j-1}+k, T^i_{j+1}+k]$. However, it is only needed that it is true when the supremum in (A.25) is attained. But this follows immediately for large N from (A.11) and (A.21), because when $|\varepsilon(t)|$ is large, the modification (4.22) is not used.

(ii) The above comments also apply in Step 3 of the proof. Here it is only needed that Lemma 4.2 is true when the supremum in (A.32) is attained.

Finally, the modification might cause some terms in the estimate of $\hat{e}_f(t|t-1)$ in Lemma A.3 to be zero. This fact just simplifies the proof.

The proof of Theorem 4.1 is thus still valid with these small modifications and the theorem is proven. □

Admittedly, the modification of the algorithm requires an upper bound on the disturbance which is not known a priori. It is of course possible to use a large K_w to assure that (4.23) is fulfilled. On the other hand, this implies that the prediction error $\varepsilon(t)$ can be large without causing any adjustment of the estimates. If β_0 is reasonably close to b_0 and the noise amplitude is small compared to the largest acceptable magnitude of the prediction error, then the modification could be of practical significance. Modifications of this sort are also common in practical algorithms.

As an example, the case $\beta_0 = b_0$ and $k = 0$ for the deterministic design will be considered. Then $R(q^{-1}) = 1$. If it is also assumed that $Q = TA^M$ and $P = 1$ as in Example 2.3, the test (4.22) can be made very simple:

$$|\varepsilon(t)| = |e_f(t)| < 2 \sup_t |w(t)|.$$

This means that an error $\varepsilon(t)$ twice the maximal noise amplitude is accepted. This is not very restrictive if the signal to noise ratio is high. It should also be noted that an error of the same magnitude as the disturbance would be expected even for known parameters, at least in the case with white noise.

Apart from the modification described in Theorem 4.3, there is one natural modification of the algorithm which will guarantee that the estimates are bounded. This is achieved by projecting the estimates into a bounded area. Such a modification is always made in practice. Similar techniques have also appeared for a long time in the stochastic approximation literature. See e.g. Albert/Gardner (1967) and Ljung (1977b). Different possibilities to make the projection exist. Below it is shown formally that one such modification will make the closed-loop system stable.

THEOREM 4.4 (*DSA-algorithm with projection*)

Consider the plant (4.1), controlled by the DSA-algorithm with deterministic or stochastic design, modified in the following way:

$$\begin{cases} \hat{b}_0'(t) = \hat{b}_0(t-1) + \left(\dfrac{\overline{u}(t-k-1)}{p_1} + \hat{\theta}^T(t-1)\,\overline{\varphi}(t-k-1)\right)\dfrac{\varepsilon(t)}{r(t)} \\ \hat{\theta}'(t) = \hat{\theta}(t-1) + \beta_0\,\overline{\varphi}(t-k-1)\,\dfrac{\varepsilon(t)}{r(t)} \end{cases} \tag{4.24}$$

$$\begin{pmatrix} \hat{b}_0(t) \\ \hat{\theta}(t) \end{pmatrix} = \begin{cases} \dfrac{C}{\left|[\hat{b}_0'(t)\;\hat{\theta}'^T(t)]\right|}\begin{pmatrix} \hat{b}_0'(t) \\ \hat{\theta}'(t) \end{pmatrix} & \text{if } \left\|\begin{pmatrix} \hat{b}_0'(t) \\ \hat{\theta}'(t) \end{pmatrix}\right\| > C \quad (4.25a) \\ \begin{pmatrix} \hat{b}_0'(t) \\ \hat{\theta}'(t) \end{pmatrix} & \text{otherwise,} \quad (4.25b) \end{cases}$$

where C is a positive constant, satisfying

$$C > 2\sqrt{\frac{\max\,(1,\, b_0/\beta_0)}{\min\,(1,\, b_0/\beta_0)}}\;\left\|\begin{pmatrix} b_0 \\ \theta \end{pmatrix}\right\|. \tag{4.26}$$

Here b_0 and θ are the true plant parameters. Assume that A1 - A3 are

satisfied and that $b_0 < 2\beta_0$. Then the closed-loop system is L^∞-stable.
□

Proof

The proof is given for the deterministic design. It is obvious that the modification implies that the parameter estimates are bounded. Theorem 4.1 can, however, not be applied straightforwardly, because the algorithm has been modified. The equations for updating the parameters are used in the proofs of Lemmas 4.2 and A.3. These lemmas will be considered separately.

Define

$$\psi^T = [b_0 \sqrt{b_0/\beta_0}\ \theta^T]$$

$$\hat{\psi}^T(t) = [\hat{b}_0(t) \sqrt{b_0/\beta_0}\ \hat{\theta}^T(t)]$$

$$\tilde{\psi}^T(t) = [\tilde{b}_0(t) \sqrt{b_0/\beta_0}\ \tilde{\theta}^T(t)]$$

and analogously $\hat{\psi}'(t)$ and $\tilde{\psi}'(t)$. We have

$$\min(1, b_0/\beta_0)(b_0^2 + |\theta|^2) \leq |\psi|^2 \leq \max(1, b_0/\beta_0)(b_0^2 + |\theta|^2) \qquad (4.27)$$

and similarly for the other ψ-vectors defined above.

Consider now those times, when the projection (4.25a) is used. It follows from (4.25a), (4.26) and (4.27) that, for some μ, $0 < \mu < 1/2$,

$$|\hat{\psi}'(t)|^2 \geq \min(1, b_0/\beta_0)(\hat{b}_0'^2(t) + |\hat{\theta}'(t)|^2) >$$

$$> \min(1, b_0/\beta_0)\ C^2 \geq \frac{1}{\mu^2} \max(1, b_0/\beta_0)(b_0^2 + |\theta|^2) \geq \frac{1}{\mu^2} |\psi|^2,$$

which implies that

$$|\psi| \leq \mu\ |\hat{\psi}'(t)| \leq \mu\ (|\tilde{\psi}'(t)| + |\psi|).$$

Hence,

$$|\psi| \leq \frac{\mu}{1-\mu} |\tilde{\psi}'(t)|. \qquad (4.28)$$

Let

$$\gamma(t) \triangleq \frac{C}{|[\hat{b}_0'(t)\ \hat{\theta}'^T(t)]|},$$

and use (4.25a), (4.28) to obtain

$$|\tilde{\psi}(t)| = \left\| \begin{pmatrix} \hat{b}_0(t) - b_0 \\ \sqrt{b_0/\beta_0}\,[\hat{\theta}(t) - \theta] \end{pmatrix} \right\| = \left\| \begin{pmatrix} \gamma(t)\ \hat{b}_0'(t) - b_0 \\ \sqrt{b_0/\beta_0}\,[\gamma(t)\ \hat{\theta}'(t) - \theta] \end{pmatrix} \right\| \leq$$

$$\leq \gamma(t)\ |\tilde{\psi}'(t)| + [1 - \gamma(t)]\ |\psi| \leq$$

$$\leq |\tilde{\psi}'(t)| - [1 - \gamma(t)] \left(|\tilde{\psi}'(t)| - \frac{\mu}{1-\mu}\ |\tilde{\psi}'(t)| \right) \leq$$

$$\leq |\tilde{\psi}'(t)| - [1 - \gamma(t)]\ \frac{1-2\mu}{1-\mu}\ |\tilde{\psi}'(t)| \leq |\tilde{\psi}'(t)|,$$

where the last step follows because $\gamma(t)$ is less than one and μ is less than 1/2. This inequality implies that Lemma 4.2 is still applicable.

The proof of Lemma A.3 remains to be discussed. If the projection (4.25a) is used, the proof now gives estimates of terms of the type $|\hat{\theta}'(t) - \hat{\theta}(t-1)|$ instead of $|\hat{\theta}(t) - \hat{\theta}(t-1)|$. But it follows from (4.25a) that

$$|\hat{\theta}(t) - \hat{\theta}(t-1)| = |\gamma(t)\ \hat{\theta}'(t) - \hat{\theta}(t-1)| \leq$$

$$\leq \gamma(t)\ |\hat{\theta}'(t) - \hat{\theta}(t-1)| + [1 - \gamma(t)]\ |\hat{\theta}(t-1)| \leq$$

$$\leq |\hat{\theta}'(t) - \hat{\theta}(t-1)| + \frac{|[\hat{b}_0'(t)\ \hat{\theta}'^T(t)]| - C}{|[\hat{b}_0'(t)\ \hat{\theta}'^T(t)]|}\ |\hat{\theta}(t-1)| \leq$$

$$\leq |\hat{\theta}'(t) - \hat{\theta}(t-1)| + \frac{|[\hat{b}_0'(t)\ \hat{\theta}'^T(t)]| - C}{C}\ |\hat{\theta}(t-1)| \leq$$

$$\leq |\hat{\theta}'(t) - \hat{\theta}(t-1)| + |[\hat{b}_0'(t)\ \hat{\theta}'^T(t)]| - C,$$

where the last step follows from the fact that the estimates are bounded by C. Use this inequality together with (4.24) and (4.6f) to obtain

$$|\hat{\theta}(t) - \hat{\theta}(t-1)| \leq |\hat{\theta}'(t) - \hat{\theta}(t-1)| + \left\| \begin{pmatrix} \hat{b}_0(t-1) \\ \hat{\theta}(t-1) \end{pmatrix} \right\| +$$

$$+ \left\| \begin{pmatrix} [\hat{\theta}(t-1) - \hat{\theta}(t-k-1)]^T \, \overline{\varphi}(t-k-1) \\ \beta_0 \, \overline{\varphi}(t-k-1) \end{pmatrix} \right\| \cdot \frac{|\varepsilon(t)|}{r(t)} - C \leq$$

$$\leq |\hat{\theta}'(t) - \hat{\theta}(t-1)| + (2C + \beta_0) \, |\overline{\varphi}(t-k-1)| \, \frac{|\varepsilon(t)|}{r(t)} .$$

It is easy to see that the extra term in the right hand side of the inequality above does not affect the proof of Lemma A.3

It is thus shown that Theorem 4.1 can be applied with these small changes and the theorem is proven. □

REMARK

The modification (4.25a) is a scale reduction, which simply assures that the norm of the vector of parameter estimates is bounded by a constant C. The condition (4.26) ensures that the projection is applied sufficiently far away from the true parameters. □

A discussion of the results obtained so far is given in Section 4.4. Now consider the DLS-algorithm.

L^∞-stability for the DLS-algorithm

It seems difficult to directly extend the stability results for the DSA-algorithm to the DLS-algorithm. Only a preliminary result is therefore given. The following theorem, which corresponds to Theorem 4.1 for the DSA-algorithm, illustrates the difficulties.

THEOREM 4.5 (DLS-algorithm with noise)

Consider the plant (4.1) controlled by the DLS-algorithm with deterministic or stochastic design. Assume that A1 - A3 are satisfied, that

b_0 is known and that

$$\sup_t \bar{\varphi}^T(t-k)\ P(t)\ \bar{\varphi}(t-k) < \infty. \tag{4.29}$$

Then the closed loop system is L^∞-stable.

Proof

As for the DSA-algorithm the proof is given for the deterministic design case. The stochastic design case is treated analogously.

Apply Lemma 4.3 to obtain

$$\tilde{\theta}^T(t)\ P^{-1}(t)\ \tilde{\theta}(t) + \sum_{s=k+1}^{t} \lambda^{t-s} \frac{\lambda}{\lambda + \bar{\varphi}^T(s-k-1)\ P(s-1)\ \bar{\varphi}(s-k-1)} \cdot \frac{\varepsilon^2(s)}{b_0^2} =$$

$$= \lambda^{t-k}\ \tilde{\theta}^T(k)\ P^{-1}(k)\ \tilde{\theta}(k) + \sum_{s=k+1}^{t} \lambda^{t-s} \frac{1}{b_0^2} \left(\frac{R}{P}\ \bar{w}(s)\right)^2.$$

The assumption (4.29) and the boundedness of the noise w(t) imply

$$\varepsilon^2(t) \leq \sum_{s=k+1}^{t} \lambda^{t-s}\ \varepsilon^2(s) \leq \frac{\lambda + \sup_t \bar{\varphi}^T(t-k)\ P(t)\ \bar{\varphi}(t-k)}{\lambda} \sum_{s=k+1}^{t} \lambda^{t-s} \cdot$$

$$\cdot \frac{\lambda}{\lambda + \bar{\varphi}^T(s-k-1)\ P(s-1)\ \bar{\varphi}(s-k-1)} \frac{\varepsilon^2(s)}{b_0^2} \leq$$

$$\leq K_1 \left[1 + \sum_{s=k+1}^{t} \lambda^{t-s} \frac{1}{b_0^2} \left(\frac{R}{P}\ \bar{w}(s)\right)^2\right] \leq K_2 \tag{4.30}$$

for some constants K_1 and K_2.

It follows from Equations (4.8 a,d,e) that

$$|\hat{y}_f(t|t-1)| = \left| b_0 \left(\frac{\overline{u(t-k-1)}}{P_1} + \hat{\theta}^T(t-1)\ \bar{\varphi}(t-k-1)\right)\right| \leq$$

$$\leq \left| b_0 \left[\left(\hat{\theta}^T(t-1) - \hat{\theta}^T(t-k-1)\right) \bar{\varphi}(t-k-1)\right]\right| + \left| \frac{QB^M}{PA^M}\ u^M(t-k-1)\right| \leq$$

$$\leq \left|\bar{\varphi}^T(t-k-2)\ P(t-1)\ \bar{\varphi}(t-k-1)\ \varepsilon(t-1)\right| + \ldots +$$

$$+ \left|\bar{\varphi}^T(t-2k-1)\ P(t-k)\ \varphi(t-k-1)\ \varepsilon(t-k)\right| + \left|\frac{QB^M}{PA^M}\ u^M(t-k-1)\right|. \quad (4.31)$$

Consider one term in the sum, i.e. for $1 \leq i \leq k$,

$$|\bar{\varphi}^T(t-k-1-i)\ P(t-i)\ \bar{\varphi}(t-k-1)\ \varepsilon(t-i)| \leq$$

$$\leq [\bar{\varphi}^T(t-k-1-i)P(t-i)\bar{\varphi}(t-k-1-i)]^{1/2}[\bar{\varphi}^T(t-k-1)P(t-i)\bar{\varphi}(t-k-1)]^{1/2}|\varepsilon(t-i)| \leq$$

$$\leq [\bar{\varphi}^T(t-k-1)\ P(t-i)\ \bar{\varphi}(t-k-1)]^{1/2}\ |\varepsilon(t-i)|, \quad (4.32)$$

where the last step follows from the fact that

$$\bar{\varphi}^T(t-k-1)\ P(t)\ \bar{\varphi}(t-k-1) \leq 1. \quad (4.33)$$

This inequality follows readily from (4.8f). Furthermore, (4.8b) implies

$$\bar{\varphi}^T(t-k-1)\ P(t-i)\ \bar{\varphi}(t-k-1) =$$

$$= \bar{\varphi}^T(t-k-1)\ P(t-i+1)\ P^{-1}(t-i+1)\ P(t-i)\ \bar{\varphi}(t-k-1) =$$

$$= \bar{\varphi}^T(t-k-1)P(t-i+1)\ [\lambda I + \bar{\varphi}(t-k-i)\bar{\varphi}^T(t-k-i)P(t-i)]\ \bar{\varphi}(t-k-1) =$$

$$= \lambda\ \bar{\varphi}^T(t-k-1)\ P(t-i+1)\ \bar{\varphi}(t-k-1) +$$

$$+ [\bar{\varphi}^T(t-k-1)\ P(t-i+1)\ \bar{\varphi}(t-k-i)]\cdot[\bar{\varphi}^T(t-k-i)\ P(t-i)\ \bar{\varphi}(t-k-1)] \leq$$

$$\leq \lambda\ \bar{\varphi}^T(t-k-1)\ P(t-i+1)\ \bar{\varphi}(t-k-1) +$$

$$+ [\bar{\varphi}^T(t-k-1)P(t-i+1)\bar{\varphi}(t-k-1)]^{1/2}\cdot[\bar{\varphi}^T(t-k-i)P(t-i+1)\bar{\varphi}(t-k-i)]^{1/2}\cdot$$

$$\cdot\ [\bar{\varphi}^T(t-k-i)\ P(t-i)\ \bar{\varphi}(t-k-i)]^{1/2}\cdot[\bar{\varphi}^T(t-k-1)\ P(t-i)\ \bar{\varphi}(t-k-1)]^{1/2}. \quad (4.34)$$

But, since $P(t-i+1) \leq \frac{1}{\lambda}\ P(t-i)$,

$$\bar{\varphi}^T(t-k-1)\ P(t-i+1)\ \bar{\varphi}(t-k-1) \leq$$

$$\leq [\bar{\varphi}^T(t-k-1)P(t-i+1)\bar{\varphi}(t-k-1)]^{1/2}\ [\frac{1}{\lambda}\ \bar{\varphi}^T(t-k-1)P(t-i)\bar{\varphi}(t-k-1)]^{1/2}.$$

Using this inequality and (4.33), (4.34) gives

$$\bar{\varphi}^T(t-k-1)\ P(t-i)\ \bar{\varphi}(t-k-1) \leq$$

$$\leq [\bar{\varphi}^T(t-k-1)P(t-i+1)\bar{\varphi}(t-k-1)]^{1/2} \cdot [\bar{\varphi}^T(t-k-1)P(t-i)\bar{\varphi}(t-k-1)]^{1/2} \cdot$$

$$\cdot [\sqrt{\lambda} + [\bar{\varphi}^T(t-k-i)\ P(t-i)\ \bar{\varphi}(t-k-i)]^{1/2}],$$

which implies that

$$\bar{\varphi}^T(t-k-1)\ P(t-i)\ \bar{\varphi}(t-k-1) \leq$$

$$\leq [\bar{\varphi}^T(t-k-1)P(t-i+1)\bar{\varphi}(t-k-1)] \cdot [\sqrt{\lambda} + [\bar{\varphi}^T(t-k-i)P(t-i)\bar{\varphi}(t-k-i)]^{1/2}]^2 \leq$$

$$\leq 2[\bar{\varphi}^T(t-k-1)P(t-i+1)\bar{\varphi}(t-k-1)] \cdot [\lambda + \bar{\varphi}^T(t-k-i)P(t-i)\bar{\varphi}(t-k-i)] \leq$$

$$\leq 2[1 + \sup_t \bar{\varphi}(t-k)P(t)\bar{\varphi}(t-k)] \cdot [\bar{\varphi}^T(t-k-1)P(t-i+1)\bar{\varphi}(t-k-1)].$$

Use this inequality recursively for $i = 1, \ldots, k$ and exploit (4.33) for $i = 1$. The result is

$$\bar{\varphi}^T(t-k-1)P(t-i)\bar{\varphi}(t-k-1) \leq 2^i[1 + \sup_t \bar{\varphi}(t-k)P(t)\varphi(t-k)]^i \leq$$

$$\leq 2^k[1 + \sup_t \bar{\varphi}^T(t-k)\ P(t)\ \bar{\varphi}(t-k)]^k, \qquad i = 1, \ldots, k.$$

But from (4.29) this is bounded, by a constant K_3 say, so that the inequalities (4.31) and (4.32) give

$$|\hat{y}_f(t|t-1)| \leq \sqrt{K_3}[|\varepsilon(t-1)| + \ldots + |\varepsilon(t-k)|] +$$

$$+ \left|\frac{QB^M}{PA^M}\ u^M(t-k-1)\right| \leq k\sqrt{K_2K_3} + \left|\frac{QB^M}{PA^M}\ u^M(t-k-1)\right|,$$

where (4.30) have been used in the last step.

The conclusion is thus that both $\varepsilon(t)$ and $\hat{y}_f(t|t-1)$ are uniformly bounded. But from (4.3) and (4.8c) it follows that

$$\frac{e(t)}{P(q^{-1})} = \frac{y(t)}{P} - \frac{y^M(t)}{P} = \frac{y_f(t)}{Q} - \frac{y^M(t)}{P} =$$

$$= \frac{1}{Q}\ [\varepsilon(t) + \hat{y}_f(t|t-1)] - \frac{y^M(t)}{P}$$

and since $Q(q^{-1})$ and $P(q^{-1})$ are asymptotically stable, $e(t)/P(q^{-1})$ is also uniformly bounded. Hence, from Lemma 4.1, $\varphi(t)$ is generated by an asymptotically stable filter with bounded inputs. Therefore $\varphi(t)$ is bounded and consequently also $y(t)$ and $u(t)$ are bounded. □

If the result above is compared with Theorem 4.1, it can be seen that the boundedness condition on the parameter estimates has been replaced by the condition (4.29). This condition is unpleasant since it cannot be verified a priori. In the case with only one unknown parameter, i.e. with $\varphi(t)$ being a scalar, the condition can be written

$$\sup_t \frac{\bar{\varphi}^2(t-k)}{\dfrac{\lambda^{t-k}}{P(k)} + \sum_{s=0}^{t-k-1} \lambda^{t-k-1-s}\, \bar{\varphi}^2(s)} < \infty .$$

This means that $\bar{\varphi}$ shall not increase arbitrarily fast compared to the weighted sum of old $\bar{\varphi}$. This is similar to, but somewhat weaker than, the condition which was used for the DSA-algorithm and which was proven in Lemma A.2. The assumption on boundedness of the parameter estimates was used in the proof. The condition (4.29) thus holds if the estimates are bounded and only one parameter is estimated.

However, when φ is a vector, the change of φ's direction makes the condition more difficult to interpret. One possibility is the following one. Let v_t^i, $i = 1, \ldots, n$ be orthonormal eigenvectors of $P^{-1}(t)$. Here n is the dimension of φ. Thus,

$$P^{-1}(t)\, v_t^i = \lambda_t^i\, v_t^i$$

and

$$P(t)\, v_t^i = \frac{1}{\lambda_t^i}\, v_t^i,$$

where $\{\lambda_t^i\}_{i=1}^n$ are the eigenvalues. Since

$$\bar{\varphi}(t-k) = \sum_{i=1}^n [\bar{\varphi}^T(t-k)\, v_t^i]\, v_t^i,$$

it follows that

$$\bar{\varphi}^T(t-k)\; P(t)\; \bar{\varphi}(t-k) = \sum_{i=1}^{n} \frac{1}{\lambda_t^i}\, [\bar{\varphi}^T(t-k)\; v_t^i]^2 .$$

But

$$\lambda_t^i = v_t^{iT} P^{-1}(t)\, v_t^i = \lambda^{t-k} v_t^{iT} P^{-1}(k)\, v_t^i + \sum_{s=0}^{t-k-1} \lambda^{t-k-1-s} [\bar{\varphi}^T(s)\; v_t^i]^2$$

so that

$$\bar{\varphi}^T(t-k) P(t) \bar{\varphi}(t-k) = \sum_{i=1}^{n} \frac{[\bar{\varphi}^T(t-k)\, v_t^i]^2}{\lambda^{t-k} v_t^{iT} P^{-1}(k)\, v_t^i + \sum_{s=0}^{t-k-1} \lambda^{t-k-1-s} [\bar{\varphi}^T(s)\, v_t^i]^2}$$

The conclusion is that a sufficient condition for (4.29) to hold is that there is a K, independent of t, such that for every t,

$$[v^T \bar{\varphi}(t)]^2 \lesssim K \left(\lambda^{t-k} + \sum_{s=0}^{t-1} \lambda^{t-1-s} [v^T \bar{\varphi}(s)]^2\right) \quad \forall\, v, \quad |v| = 1.$$

This condition is analogous to the interpretation in the scalar case. It says that the growth of $\bar{\varphi}$ in an arbitrary direction must be bounded by the weighted sum of old components of $\bar{\varphi}$ in that same direction.

The conclusion of the discussion above is that it is necessary to examine the condition (4.29) more thoroughly in order to derive results corresponding to Theorems 4.2, 4.3 and 4.4 for the DSA-algorithm or to look for other methods of proving stability.

4.3. Convergence in the disturbance-free case

An important motivation for the L^∞-stability investigation is that a boundedness condition is needed in the convergence analysis. This was pointed out in Chapter 2 and in the beginning of this chapter. The results of the preceeding section will now be used to solve the convergence problem in the deterministic case. It will thus be shown that part of the state of the closed-loop system, namely the output error $e = y - y^M$, tends to zero if the disturbance w is equal to zero.

Consider first the DSA-algorithm. The following result follows from Theorem 4.2.

THEOREM 4.6 (DSA-algorithm without noise)

Consider the plant (4.1) with no noise, i.e. $w(t) = 0$. Let the plant be controlled by the DSA-algorithm for deterministic design, (4.6). Assume that A1 - A3 hold, that $b_0 < 2\beta_0$ and $\alpha > 0$ and that the command input $u^M(t)$ is uniformly bounded. Then the output error converges to zero, i.e.

$$y(t) - y^M(t) \to 0, \quad t \to \infty. \qquad \square$$

Proof

It follows from Lemma 4.2 that

$$\frac{\varepsilon^2(t)}{r(t)} \to 0, \quad t \to \infty$$

and so, because $r(t)$ is bounded from Theorem 4.2,

$$\varepsilon(t) \to 0, \quad t \to \infty.$$

Furthermore, as in the proof of Lemma A.3 in Appendix A,

$$|\hat{e}_f(t|t-1)| \leqslant$$

$$\leqslant |\hat{b}_0(t-1)|\ \beta_0 \left| \bar{\varphi}^T(t-k-2)\ \frac{\varepsilon(t-1)}{r(t-1)} + \ldots + \bar{\varphi}^T(t-2k-1)\ \frac{\varepsilon(t-k)}{r(t-k)} \right| |\bar{\varphi}(t-k-1)|.$$

Here $\hat{b}_0(t-1)$ and $\bar{\varphi}(t)$ are bounded from Lemma 4.2 and Theorem 4.2. Also note that $r(t) \geqslant \alpha > 0$ from the assumptions. It thus follows that

$$\hat{e}_f(t|t-1) \to 0, \quad t \to \infty.$$

Consequently, since $Q(q^{-1})$ is asymptotically stable,

$$y(t) - y^M(t) = \frac{P(q^{-1})}{Q(q^{-1})}\ e_f(t) = \frac{P(q^{-1})}{Q(q^{-1})}\ [\varepsilon(t) + \hat{e}_f(t|t-1)] \to 0, \ t \to \infty$$

and the theorem is proven. $\square$

The result above can be applied to modified versions of the schemes by Ionescu/Monopoli and Åström/Wittenmark, described in Chapter 2. It is also possible to infer the convergence of the output error for the scheme by Bénéjean. Only minor changes are needed in the analysis. This means that the convergence problem is solved for several schemes without noise. In contrast to earlier convergence results for discrete time MRAS, the result does not require any a priori assumption of boundedness of the closed-loop signals.

The situation for the least squares version of the general algorithm is, however, not that pleasing, as can be seen in the following theorem.

THEOREM 4.7 (DLS-algorithm without noise)

Consider the plant (4.1) without noise, i.e. $w(t) = 0$. Let the plant be controlled by the DLS-algorithm for deterministic design, (4.8). Assume that A1 - A3 hold and that b_0 is known. Further assume that $k = 0$ and that

$$\sup_t \bar{\varphi}^T(t)\; P(t)\; \bar{\varphi}(t) < \infty.$$

Then the output error converges to zero, i.e.

$$y(t) - y^M(t) \to 0, \quad t \to \infty. \qquad \square$$

Proof

It readily follows from Lemma 4.3 that

$$\varepsilon(t) \to 0, \quad t \to \infty.$$

But $k = 0$ implies that $e_f(t) = \varepsilon(t)$ as can be seen from (4.8 d,e). The conclusion then follows as in Theorem 4.6. □

It is seen that the unpleasant condition (4.29) is still required. Furthermore, it is assumed that $k = 0$. This condition can be avoided by modifying the estimation scheme and control law. If delayed parameter estimates are used in (4.8 d,e), it is possible to have

$e_f(t) = \varepsilon(t)$ and the proof holds for the case $k \neq 0$ too. The conclusion is that the analysis for the DLS-algorithm is not as complete as for the DSA-algorithm and that further work on the DLS-algorithm is needed.

Finally, it should be mentioned that there is one problem that has not been treated here. This is to consider convergence not only of the output error, but of another part of the state vector, namely the parameter estimates. To make this analysis meaningful, it is necessary to assume that the number of parameters is correctly chosen. Note that this has not been required so far. We will, however, not elaborate on this problem. Let it suffice to note that some kind of persistently exciting condition on the command input is sufficient for the estimation errors to tend to zero. See e.g. Kudva/Narendra (1974).

4.4. Results on other configurations

The stability analysis given in the previous sections has been concerned with a specific class of algorithms. In particular, some minor changes of the algorithms were needed in order to apply the results. Therefore a few possible extensions of the analysis are indicated in this section.

Other model structures

The structure of the model for the DSA- and DLS-algorithms was chosen in a particular way. The model reference adaptive systems provided the motivation. The characteristic property of the MRAS structure is that the model contains the unknown parameters b_0 and θ as a *product*, see (4.4). This is in contrast to most model structures used for identification and self-tuning regulators. For example, the self-tuning controller considered in Example 2.3 uses a model which is *linear* in the unknown parameters. In the general case, a model which is linear in the unknown parameters can be obtained in the following way. Let θ denote b_0 times the previous θ-vector and write (4.4) as

$$e_f(t) = q^{-(k+1)}\left(b_0 \frac{\overline{u}(t)}{P_1} + \theta^T \overline{\varphi}(t)\right) + \frac{QR}{TA^M P} w(t). \tag{4.33}$$

This model suggests an alternative to the DSA-algorithm. The new algorithm can be written analogously with equation (4.6) as:

- estimation:

$$\left\{\begin{array}{ll} \hat{\theta}(t) = \hat{\theta}(t-1) + \overline{\varphi}(t-k-1) \dfrac{\varepsilon(t)}{r(t)} & (4.34a) \\ r(t) = \lambda\, r(t-1) + |\overline{\varphi}(t-k-1)|^2 + \alpha & (4.34b) \\ \varepsilon(t) = e_f(t) - \hat{e}_f(t|t-1) & (4.34c) \\ \hat{e}_f(t|t-1) = \beta_0 \dfrac{\overline{u}(t-k-1)}{P_1} + \hat{\theta}^T(t-1)\, \overline{\varphi}(t-k-1) & (4.34d) \end{array}\right.$$

- control:

$$\frac{\overline{u}(t)}{P_1} = - \frac{1}{\beta_0} \hat{\theta}^T(t)\, \overline{\varphi}(t) \tag{4.34e}$$

REMARK

Note that an a priori estimate β_0 of b_0 is still used. Also notice that the last element of θ is known to be unity, but it is necessary to estimate it because β_0 might be chosen different from b_0. □

The key result, which is needed in the stability proofs, is Lemma 4.2. It will be shown that the lemma still holds for the algorithm above if $k = 0$. Define

$$\tilde{\theta}(t) = \hat{\theta}(t) - \frac{\beta_0}{b_0} \theta.$$

Write (4.34a) in terms of $\tilde{\theta}$ and multiply from the left by its transpose. This gives for $k = 0$

$$|\tilde{\theta}(t)|^2 = |\tilde{\theta}(t-1)|^2 + 2\, \tilde{\theta}^T(t-1)\, \overline{\varphi}(t-1) \frac{\varepsilon(t)}{r(t)} + |\overline{\varphi}(t-1)|^2 \frac{\varepsilon^2(t)}{r^2(t)} \leqslant$$

$$\leqslant |\tilde{\theta}(t-1)|^2 + \frac{1}{r(t)} [2\, \tilde{\theta}^T(t-1)\, \overline{\varphi}(t-1)\, \varepsilon(t) + \varepsilon^2(t)].$$

It follows from (4.33) and (4.34 c,d,e) that

$$\varepsilon(t) = e_f(t) - \hat{e}_f(t|t-1) = b_0 \frac{\overline{u}(t-1)}{P_1} + \theta^T \overline{\varphi}(t-1) + \frac{R}{P}\overline{w}(t) -$$

$$- \left(\beta_0 \frac{\overline{u}(t-1)}{P_1} + \hat{\theta}^T(t-1)\,\overline{\varphi}(t-1)\right) =$$

$$= \left(\frac{b_0}{\beta_0} - 1\right)\left(\beta_0 \frac{\overline{u}(t-1)}{P_1} + \hat{\theta}^T(t-1)\,\overline{\varphi}(t-1)\right) -$$

$$- \frac{b_0}{\beta_0}\left(\hat{\theta}(t-1) - \frac{\beta_0}{b_0}\theta\right)^T \overline{\varphi}(t-1) + \frac{R}{P}\overline{w}(t) =$$

$$= - \frac{b_0}{\beta_0}\tilde{\theta}^T(t-1)\,\overline{\varphi}(t-1) + \frac{R}{P}\overline{w}(t).$$

Inserting this expression for $\varepsilon(t)$ in the inequality above gives

$$|\tilde{\theta}(t)|^2 \leq |\tilde{\theta}(t-1)|^2 + \frac{1}{r(t)}\left[2\,\frac{\beta_0}{b_0}\left(\frac{R}{P}\overline{w}(t) - \varepsilon(t)\right)\varepsilon(t) + \varepsilon^2(t)\right] =$$

$$= |\tilde{\theta}(t-1)|^2 + \frac{1}{r(t)}\left[2\,\frac{\beta_0}{b_0}\,\frac{R}{P}\overline{w}(t)\,\varepsilon(t) - \left(2\,\frac{\beta_0}{b_0} - 1\right)\varepsilon^2(t)\right].$$

Define

$$c = \frac{\beta_0}{b_0} - \frac{1}{2},$$

which is positive under the conditions of Lemma 4.2. It then follows that

$$|\tilde{\theta}(t)|^2 \leq |\tilde{\theta}(t-1)|^2 +$$

$$+ \frac{1}{r(t)}\left[- \left(\sqrt{c}\,\varepsilon(t) - \frac{1}{\sqrt{c}}\,\frac{\beta_0}{b_0}\,\frac{R}{P}\overline{w}(t)\right)^2 - c\,\varepsilon^2(t) + \frac{1}{c}\left(\frac{\beta_0}{b_0}\,\frac{R}{P}\,\overline{w}(t)\right)^2\right] \leq$$

$$\leq |\tilde{\theta}(t-1)|^2 - c\,\frac{\varepsilon^2(t)}{r(t)} + \frac{1}{cr(t)}\left(\frac{\beta_0}{b_0}\right)^2\left(\frac{R}{P}\overline{w}(t)\right)^2.$$

The conclusion is that the lemma is still true for the new algorithm, provided $k = 0$. In this case it is thus possible to derive stability results corresponding to Theorems 4.1 - 4.4. However, it is not straightforward to show that Lemma 4.2 also holds for the case $k \neq 0$. It is thus an open question whether the MRAS structure used in the

DSA-algorithm is advantageous for the case $k \neq 0$. The difficulties in the stability analysis for the algorithm (4.34) indicates this, but on the other hand no significant differences have appeared in simulations. Similarly it may perhaps be useful to apply the MRAS-type of model structure in other cases.

Non-minimum phase systems

A characteristic feature of the schemes considered is that the process zeros are cancelled. This implies that only minimum phase systems can be treated. The underlying design method with cancellation of zeros was chosen because it gives a simple adaptive scheme. A convenient *implicit* scheme (i.e. with estimation of *controller* parameters) for nonminimum phase systems seems, however, more difficult to give. One possibility to solve the problem is to consider *explicit* schemes instead. This means that the plant parameters are estimated directly and the controller parameters are calculated from these estimates. See Åström et al. (1978).

A possibility to control nonminimum phase plants with an implicit scheme without cancellation of zeros is discussed in Clarke/Gawthrop (1975). The self-tuning controller described in Example 2.5 is used with the polynomial Q (in their notation) in the definition of the generalized error different from zero. This case is not covered by the analysis so far. See Example 2.5.

The case $Q \neq 0$ can however be treated in the following way. Change the notation in Example 2.5 into

$$\phi(t) = A^M(q^{-1})\, y(t) - B^M(q^{-1})\, u^M(t-k-1) + C^M(q^{-1})\, u(t-k-1),$$

where C^M is equal to Q in the original notation. When $C^M \neq 0$, the model in Example 2.5 changes into

$$\phi(t) = \frac{1}{C}\, q^{-(k+1)}\Big((b_0\, BR + CC^M)\, u(t) + Sy(t) - CB^M\, u^M(t)\Big) + Rv(t).$$

Denote by c_0 the constant term in C^M and rewrite the expression for $\phi(t)$ as

$$\phi(t) = \frac{1}{C} q^{-(k+1)}(b_0 + c_0)\left[u(t) + \frac{b_0 \; BR + CC^M - (b_0 + c_0)}{b_0 + c_0} u(t) + \right.$$

$$\left. + \frac{S}{b_0 + c_0} y(t) - \frac{C}{b_0 + c_0} B^M u^M(t)\right] + R\, v(t) \triangleq$$

$$\triangleq \frac{1}{C} q^{-(k+1)}(b_0 + c_0) \; [u(t) + \theta^T \varphi(t)] + R\, v(t),$$

where θ and $\varphi(t)$ are defined as for the DSA-algorithm with estimated observer. This model is analogous with the model (4.10) for the DSA-algorithm. It is therefore possible to conclude that the stability results hold for Clarke's and Gawthrop's algorithm if the "MRAS--structure" in the DSA-algorithm is used. There is, however, one condition that has to be fulfilled in order to apply the results. This is that the φ-vector is generated from $\phi(t)$ and bounded signals through stable filters. Compare with Lemma 4.1. It is easy to check that this is the case if the polynomial $(AC^M + b_0BA^M)$ is stable. This polynomial is in fact part of the closed-loop characteristic polynomial when the underlying design scheme is used for known parameters. The success of the scheme will thus heavily depend on the polynomials A^M and C^M. This fact is also discussed in Clarke/Gawthrop (1975).

4.5. Discussion

Different aspects of the stability results obtained in the previous sections will be discussed in this section. The discussion is limited to the DSA-algorithm, because the results on the DLS-algorithm are only fragmentary.

Consider first the disturbance-free case. Theorems 4.2 and 4.6 give a fairly complete picture of how the algorithms behave. Convergence of the output error to zero is proved without any a priori assumption of boundedness of closed-loop signals. Such a condition is usually required in convergence analysis of MRAS schemes also in the absence of noise. A notable exception is the globally stable continuous time scheme in Feuer/Morse (1977).

In the case with disturbances it has been demonstrated that some additional assumptions are needed to guarantee global stability. The approach taken here is to assume that the parameter estimates are bounded and two different means to ensure this were considered in Theorems 4.3 and 4.4. Another possibility is to put more conditions on the noise and/or command signal. It does not seem unreasonable that some kind of persistently exciting condition (see e.g. Åström/Bohlin (1965), Kudva/Narendra (1974)) might be sufficient to ensure the boundedness of the parameter estimates. This is however still an open problem. It should finally be pointed out that the case with decreasing gains ($\lambda = 1$) in the estimation algorithm has not been treated at all. This means that it is not possible to combine the stability results presented here with results concerning the asymptotic behaviour of the algorithms as given e.g. by Ljung (1977a).

Some comments should also be made on the structure of the estimation scheme. A model structure which is *bilinear* in the unknown parameters is used. It was noted in the previous section that it is not straightforward to extend the stability results to models which are *linear* in the unknown parameters. This is an interesting observation which perhaps deserves further investigation.

Both the DSA-algorithm and the algorithm in the preceeding section based on a model which is linear in the parameters suffer from a condition on the a priori estimate β_0 of b_0. It would of course be desirable to eliminate this condition. A straightforward solution would be to estimate b_0 in the model (4.33). The control law would then look like (4.34e) with β_0 replaced by the estimate $\hat{b}_0(t)$ of b_0. Difficulties will appear if $\hat{b}_0(t)$ is very small or has the wrong sign. In particular, the control law is undefined if $\hat{b}_0(t)$ is equal to zero. Although the scheme can behave well in practise, the stability analysis will be difficult. This approach is therefore left with these remarks.

Finally, the general assumptions introduced in Section 4.1 will be discussed. The assumption that the time delay is known seems difficult to overcome, at least in the theoretical analysis. The minimum phase assumption is a consequence of the choice of design method. It is naturally of interest to investigate the properties of algorithms which are capable of controlling nonminimum phase systems, see e.g. Åström et al. (1978) and Åström (1979). It seems that such analysis has not been carried out so far. It is also desirable to relax the condition that the orders of the plant model are not underestimated. It would be valuable to have results concerning the control of higher-order or nonlinear plants. This seems to be an unexplored area.

5. STABILITY OF CONTINUOUS TIME CONTROLLERS

It was briefly indicated in Chapter 3 that a boundedness condition is essential in the analysis of continuous time MRAS. It is easy to prove that the output error converges to zero when the pole excess is one or two, see Gilbart et al. (1970) and Monopoli (1973). However, boundedness of the closed-loop signals has been assumed to prove convergence in the general case. See Monopoli (1974), Narendra and Valavani (1977), Feuer et al. (1978). Recently Morse (1979) presented a rigorous convergence proof in the noisefree case without requiring closed loop stability.

In this chapter some stability results will be given for the general adaptive algorithm described in Chapter 3. The continuous time problem is similar to the discrete time problem. The discussion of different approaches in the beginning of Chapter 4 thus also applies to continuous time systems. The results given in this chapter are analogous to those for discrete time systems in Chapter 4.

The algorithm considered is defined in Section 5.1, which also contains some preliminary results. The main results on L^{∞}-stability are given in Section 5.2. The implications of the stability results for the convergence in the disturbance-free case is examined in Section 5.3. In particular, the convergence problem for MRAS is solved.

5.1. Preliminaries

The algorithms considered were described in Section 3.2. For easy reference, some of the equations are given below.

Plant model

The plant is described by

$$y(t) = \frac{b_0\ B(p)}{A(p)}\ u(t) + v(t) = \frac{b_0(p^m + b_1 p^{m-1} + \ldots + b_m)}{p^n + a_1 p^{n-1} + \ldots + a_n}\ u(t) + v(t), \tag{5.1}$$

where v(t) is a disturbance, which cannot be measured.

Reference model

The desired response is characterized by

$$y^M(t) = \frac{B^M(p)}{A^M(p)}\ u^M(t) = \frac{b_0^M\ p^m + \ldots + b_m^M}{p^n + a_1^M\ p^{n-1} + \ldots + a_n^M}\ u^M(t). \tag{5.2}$$

where A^M is asymptotically stable and u^M is the command input.

Filtered error

The filtered error is defined by

$$e_f(t) = \frac{Q(p)}{P(p)}\ e(t) = \frac{Q(p)}{P_1(p)\ P_2(p)}\ [y(t) - y^M(t)], \tag{5.3}$$

where

$$Q(p) = p^{n+n_T-1} + q_1\ p^{n+n_T-2} + \ldots + q_{n+n_T-1}$$

$$P_1(p) = p^{n-m-1} + p_{11}\ p^{n-m-2} + \ldots + p_{1(n-m-1)}$$

$$P_2(p) = p^{m+n_T} + p_{21}\ p^{m+n_T-1} + \ldots + p_{2(m+n_T)}$$

are all asymptotically stable polynomials.

Observer polynomial

The observer polynomial

$$T(p) = p^{n_T} + t_1\ p^{n_T-1} + \ldots + t_{n_T}, \quad n_T \geq n-m-1$$

is assumed asymptotically stable.

Estimation model

The estimation model is given by

$$e_f(t) = b_0\ \frac{\overline{u(t)}}{P_1} + b_0\ \theta^T\ \overline{\varphi}(t) + \frac{AR}{P}\ \overline{v}(t), \tag{5.4}$$

where '$\overline{}$' denotes filtering by Q/TA^M and

$$\varphi^T(t) = \left[\frac{p^{m+n_T-1}}{P} u(t), \ldots, \frac{u(t)}{P}, \frac{p^{n-1}}{P} y(t), \ldots, \frac{y(t)}{P}, -\frac{TB^M}{P} u^M(t)\right]. \tag{5.5}$$

The algorithm analysed is called the *CSA-algorithm* (Continuous time, Stochastic Approximation). The estimation scheme is inspired by the stochastic approximation method used in discrete time. The structure of the estimator is analogous to the MRAS algorithms described in Chapter 3. The CSA-algorithm is defined as follows.

CSA-ALGORITHM

- estimation:

$$\begin{cases} \dot{\hat{b}}_0(t) = \left(\frac{\overline{u(t)}}{P_1} + \hat{\theta}^T(t)\,\overline{\varphi}(t)\right)\frac{\varepsilon(t)}{r(t)} & (5.6a) \\ \dot{\hat{\theta}}(t) = \overline{\varphi}(t)\,\frac{\varepsilon(t)}{r(t)} & (5.6b) \\ \dot{r}(t) = -\lambda r(t) + |\overline{\varphi}(t)|^2 + \alpha(t); \quad \lambda > 0; & (5.6c) \\ \qquad \begin{matrix} \lambda r_{min} \leqslant \alpha(t) \leqslant \overline{\alpha},\ r(t) \leqslant r_{min} \\ 0 \leqslant \alpha(t) \leqslant \overline{\alpha},\ r(t) > r_{min} \end{matrix}\ ,\ r(0) \geqslant r_{min} > 0 & \\ \varepsilon(t) = e_f(t) - \hat{e}_f(t) & (5.6d) \\ \hat{e}_f(t) = \hat{b}_0(t)\left(\frac{\overline{u(t)}}{P_1} + \hat{\theta}^T(t)\,\overline{\varphi}(t)\right) & (5.6e) \end{cases}$$

- control:

$$\frac{\overline{u(t)}}{P_1(p)} = -\left(\frac{P_1(0)}{P_1(p)}\,\hat{\theta}^T(t)\right)\overline{\varphi}(t) \tag{5.6f}$$

□

REMARK 1

The estimation scheme is analogous to the stochastic approximation algorithm for discrete time. Compare with the DSA-algorithm in Chapter

4. The denominator $r(t)$ makes the scheme different from those usually used in MRAS, cf. Chapter 3. Note that the case with decreasing gain in the estimation algorithm ($\lambda = 0$) is *not* considered. Compare with the discussion of the DSA-algorithm. The purpose of $\alpha(t)$ is to prevent $r(t)$ from approaching zero. Also note that when the pole excess is equal to one, $P_1(p)$ is a constant and (5.6 a,f) imply that $\dot{\hat{b}}_0(t) = 0$. In this case it is thus not necessary to estimate b_0. It also follows from (5.6 d,e) that $\varepsilon(t) = e_f(t)$. □

REMARK 2

The modification proposed in Section 3.4 is used. The signals are thus filtered by the transfer function Q/TA^M. It is therefore not necessary to introduce any positive real condition. It can also be expected that the modification has a beneficial effect on the transient properties of the algorithm as was found in the discrete time case. No simulation studies have, however, been made. □

REMARK 3

Notice that the control law (5.6f) does not contain any differentiators. The control law is *not* the same as the commonly used control law (3.13). The control laws (5.6f) and (3.13) are, however, asymptotically equivalent. The important property of the control law (5.6f) is that $e_f(t)$ and $\hat{e}_f(t)$ are linear in $\overline{\varphi}(t)$. This is exploited in the proofs. It is not clear whether this modification is significant or just a technicality. The effects of different choices of control law are illustrated in a simple numerical example below. □

EXAMPLE 5.1

Consider a first order plant, given by

$$y(t) = \frac{b_0}{p + a} u(t).$$

The reference model is

$$y^M(t) = \frac{B^M(p)}{A^M(p)} u^M(t) = \frac{b^M}{p + a^M} u^M(t).$$

The algorithm in Example 3.5 is used with the polynomials

$$T = p + t_1$$
$$P_1 = A^M$$
$$P_2 = T$$
$$Q = P = P_1 P_2.$$

The expression corresponding to (3.5) is then

$$e_f(t) = b_0 \frac{u(t)}{A^M} + b_0 (r_1 - t_1) \frac{u(t)}{TA^M} + s_0 \frac{y(t)}{TA^M} - \frac{B^M}{A^M} u^M(t) =$$

$$= b_0 \frac{u(t)}{A^M} + b_0 \theta^T \overline{\varphi}(t).$$

Here

$$R(p) = p + r_1$$
$$S(p) = s_0.$$

The parameters b_0 and θ are estimated as in the CSA-algorithm. The numerical values of the different parameters are given in Table 5.1.

Table 5.1. Parameter values used in the simulations.

Parameter	a	b_0	a^M	b^M	t_1	λ	$\alpha(t)$
Value	1.0	1.0	2.0	1.0	2.0	5.0	0.1

Since the pole excess of the plant is equal to one, it is possible to use the control law (3.12), which sets $\hat{e}_f(t)$ to zero. The control law is given by

$$u(t) = - A^M(p) [\hat{\theta}^T(t) \overline{\varphi}(t)]. \tag{5.7}$$

Although it is possible to use this control law in this first order example, it is interesting to compare with the results when using other control laws, which are designed to avoid differentiators when the pole excess is larger than one. The commonly used control law (3.13) is given by

$$u(t) = - \hat{\theta}^T(t) [A^M(p) \overline{\varphi}(t)]. \tag{5.8}$$

The control law (5.6f) used in the CSA-algorithm is

$$u(t) = - A^M(p) \left[\left(\frac{a^M}{A^M(p)} \hat{\theta}^T(t)\right) \bar{\varphi}(t)\right]. \tag{5.9}$$

The closed-loop system was simulated using the different control laws given above. The initial values of the parameters were zero except $\hat{b}_0(0)$ which was equal to two. The initial value of r(t) was one. The simulation results are shown in Figures 5.1, 5.2, and 5.3 for $u^M(t)$ being a square wave. It is seen that the control law (5.7) gives the fastest convergence of the regulator at the price of larger control inputs. It can also be noticed that there are hardly any differences between the control laws (5.8) and (5.9). □

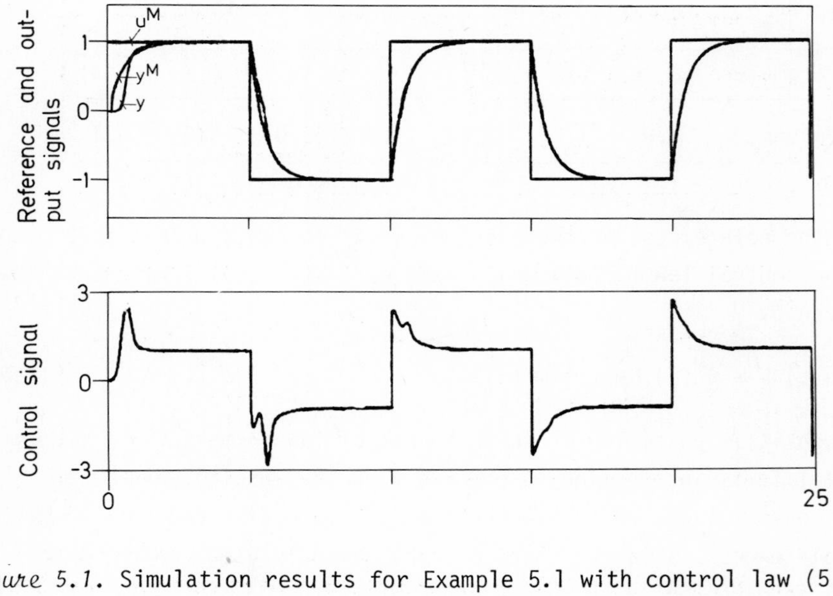

Figure 5.1. Simulation results for Example 5.1 with control law (5.7).

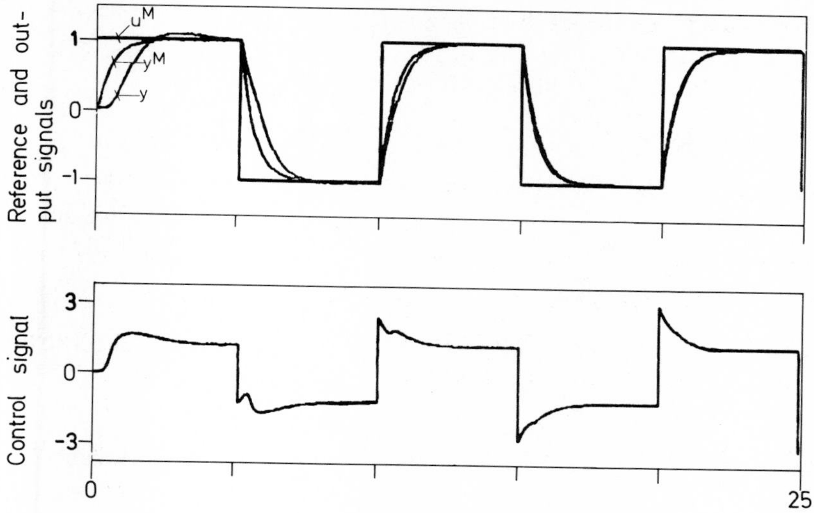

Figure 5.2. Simulation results for example 5.1 with control law (5.8).

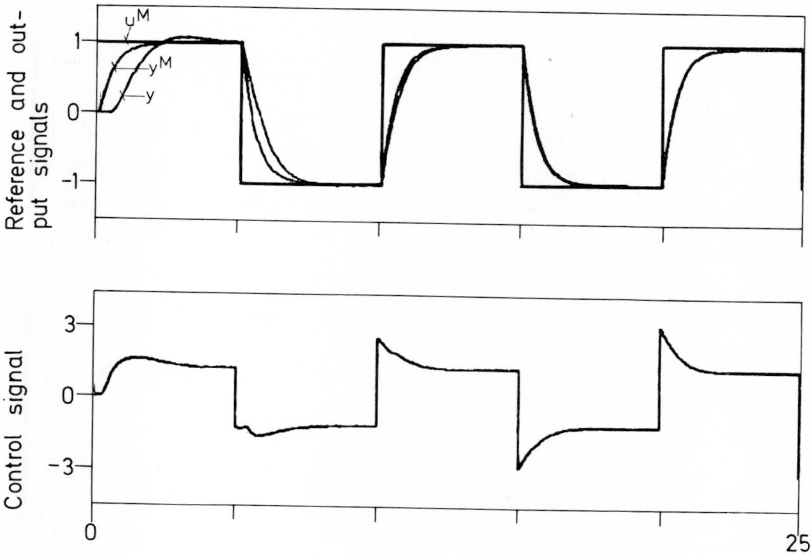

Figure 5.3. Simulation results for Example 5.1 with control law (5.9).

The following general assumptions are made:

A1) The number of poles n and zeros m are known and $m \leq n-1$.

A2) The parameter b_0 is nonzero and its sign is known. Without loss of generality b_0 is assumed positive.

A3) The plant is minimum phase, i.e. the zeros of the polynomial B(p) lie in the open left half plane.

A4) There exists a solution to the differential equations describing the closed-loop system such that $\bar{\varphi}(t)$ is continuous.

The assumptions A1 - A3 were introduced in Section 3.2 and discussed there. Juste note that if only an upper bound on n (or m) is known, the plant equation can be put into the form of (5.1) with known n and m just by multiplying A and B by factors $(p+\alpha)$. The condition A3 will not be violated by this operation if $\alpha > 0$. The condition A4 is of technical nature. It does not seem to be very restrictive. For example, it can easily be shown that the closed-loop system can be written as a differential equation

$$\dot{x}(t) = f\,[\,x(t),\, t\,]$$

where $f \in C^1$ if the noise v(t) is continuous. The existence and continuity of the solution then follows from well-known theorems for ordinary differential equations and A4 is satisfied. We will not, however, go into these details.

Finally a lemma of independent interest will be given.

LEMMA 5.1

Let $\tilde{b}_0(t)$ and $\tilde{\theta}(t)$ be defined as in Chapter 3. Then the following holds for the CSA-algorithm:

$$\frac{d}{dt}\left(\tilde{b}_0^2(t) + b_0\, \tilde{\theta}^T(t)\, \tilde{\theta}(t)\right) \leq -\frac{\varepsilon^2(t)}{r(t)} + \frac{1}{r(t)}\left(\frac{AR}{P}\,\bar{v}(t)\right)^2 \qquad (5.10)$$

□

Proof

The equations (5.6a) and (5.6b) can equivalently be written in terms of $\dot{\tilde{b}}_0$ and $\dot{\tilde{\theta}}$. Then

$$\tilde{b}_0(t)\ \dot{\tilde{b}}_0(t) = \frac{\tilde{b}_0(t)\ \varepsilon(t)}{r(t)} \left(\frac{\overline{u}(t)}{P_1} + \hat{\theta}^T(t)\ \overline{\varphi}(t)\right)$$

$$\tilde{\theta}^T(t)\ \dot{\tilde{\theta}}(t) = \tilde{\theta}^T(t)\ \overline{\varphi}(t)\ \frac{\varepsilon(t)}{r(t)}$$

which from (5.4) and (5.6 d,e) implies

$$\frac{d}{dt}\left(\tilde{b}_0^2(t) + b_0\ \tilde{\theta}^T(t)\ \tilde{\theta}(t)\right) =$$

$$= 2\ \frac{\varepsilon(t)}{r(t)} \left[\tilde{b}_0(t)\left(\frac{\overline{u}(t)}{P_1} + \hat{\theta}^T(t)\ \overline{\varphi}(t)\right) + b_0\ \tilde{\theta}^T(t)\ \overline{\varphi}(t)\right] =$$

$$= 2\ \frac{\varepsilon(t)}{r(t)} \left(\frac{AR}{P}\ \overline{v}(t) - \varepsilon(t)\right) =$$

$$= \frac{1}{r(t)} \left[-\ \varepsilon^2(t) + \left(\frac{AR}{P}\ \overline{v}(t)\right)^2 - \left(\varepsilon(t) - \frac{AR}{P}\ \overline{v}(t)\right)^2\right] \leq$$

$$\leq -\ \frac{\varepsilon^2(t)}{r(t)} + \frac{1}{r(t)} \left(\frac{AR}{P}\ \overline{v}(t)\right)^2.$$

□

5.2. L^∞-stability

Some results on L^∞-stability for the CSA-algorithm will be given in this section. They correspond to the results in Section 4.2 for discrete time. The presentation will be kept short. Refer to Section 4.2 for a discussion of the problems and ideas behind the proofs. Since L^∞-stability is considered, it is natural to assume that the command and disturbance signals are bounded. It is convenient to make the following

DEFINITION

The closed-loop system is said to be *L^∞-stable* if uniformly bounded command (u^M) and disturbance (v) signals give uniformly bounded input (u) and output (y) signals. □

The main result is given by the following theorem. It corresponds to Theorem 4.1 in discrete time and the technique used in the proof is very similar.

THEOREM 5.1 (CSA-algorithm with noise)

Consider the plant (5.1) controlled by the CSA-algorithm. Assume that assumptions A1 - A4 are satisfied and that the parameter estimates are uniformly bounded. Then the closed-loop system is L^∞-stable. □

Proof

The proof is given in Appendix B. □

Corollary

Instead of (5.6f), let the control law be given by

$$\frac{\overline{u}(t)}{P_1(p)} = -\left[G(p)\ \hat{\theta}^T(t)\right]\overline{\varphi}(t), \tag{5.11}$$

where G(p) is an asymptotically stable transfer function with pole excess greater than or equal to n - m - 1 and steady state gain equal to one. Then the theorem is still true. □

Proof

The only properties of the transfer function $P_1(0)/P_1(p)$ that are used in the proof are that the steady state gain is one, that $P_1(p)$ is asymptotically stable and that degree $(P_1) \geq$ degree $(P_1(0)) + n - m - 1$. The proof therefore still holds if (5.11) is used. □

REMARK

If r(t) is replaced by $\alpha + |\overline{\varphi}(t)|^2$, α positive constant, in the estimation part, the conclusion of the theorem is still true. □

Theorem 5.1 can be specialized in different ways. The origin of the stability investigations were the problems with MRAS. In that case noise is generally not included in the problem formulation and Theorem 5.1 can be specialized to give the solution.

THEOREM 5.2 (*CSA-algorithm without noise*)

Consider the plant (5.1) with no noise, i.e. v(t) = 0, controlled by the CSA-algorithm. Assume that assumptions A1 - A4 are satisfied. Then the closed-loop system is L^∞-stable. □

Proof

The boundedness of the parameter estimates follows immediately from Lemma 5.1, and Theorem 5.1 can be applied. □

Recall from Section 3.3 that the general structure includes several MRAS, e.g. the ones by Monopoli, Feuer/Morse and Narendra/Valavani. If the estimation algorithm in these schemes are chosen as the one in (5.6 a-e) - or as in the remark following Theorem 5.1 - and if the control law (5.6f) is used, the boundedness follows from Theorem 5.2. The complicated modifications introduced by Feuer and Morse (1977) should thus not be necessary to obtain stability. Such modifications could of course still have effect on e.g. convergence rates.

Theorem 5.2 gives a fairly satisfactory stability result for the deterministic case. A natural question is whether it is possible to extend the result in Theorem 5.2 to the case of disturbances which are not zero. The assumption of bounded estimates in Theorem 5.1 is, however, difficult to verify a priori. In analogy with the discrete time case, two possibilities to modify the algorithm to ensure bounded estimates are presented below.

THEOREM 5.3 (CSA-algorithm with conditional updating)

Consider the plant (5.1) controlled by the CSA-algorithm, modified in the following way:

$$\left.\begin{aligned} \dot{\hat{b}}_0(t) &= 0 \\ \dot{\hat{\theta}}(t) &= 0 \end{aligned}\right\} \quad \text{if} \quad |\varepsilon(t)| < K_v, \tag{5.12}$$

where K_v is a positive constant, satisfying

$$\sup_t \left| \frac{AR}{P} \, \overline{v}(t) \right| \leq K_v. \tag{5.13}$$

Assume that A1 - A4 are satisfied. Then the closed-loop system is L^∞-stable. □

Proof

Two problems have to be considered in order to apply Theorem 5.1. It must be shown that the estimates are bounded and the consequences on Theorem 5.1 of the modification (5.12) must be examined. First, Lemma 5.1 gives

$$\frac{d}{dt}\left(\tilde{b}_0^2(t) + b_0 \, \tilde{\theta}^T(t) \, \tilde{\theta}(t)\right) \leq -\frac{\varepsilon^2(t)}{r(t)} + \frac{1}{r(t)} \left(\frac{AR}{P} \, \overline{v}(t)\right)^2 \leq 0 \tag{5.14}$$

if

$$|\varepsilon(t)| \geq K_v \geq \left| \frac{AR}{P} \, \overline{v}(t) \right|.$$

On the other hand, it follows from (5.12) that

$$\frac{d}{dt}\left(\tilde{b}_0^2(t) + b_0 \, \tilde{\theta}^T(t) \, \tilde{\theta}(t)\right) \leq 0$$

if

$$|\varepsilon(t)| < K_v.$$

The parameter estimates are thus bounded.

For the second problem, the following changes are needed:

(i) In Step 2 of the proof, Lemma 5.1 is used in the derivation of

(B.30). However, if the function $1_\Omega(t)$ is defined as

$$1_\Omega(t) = \begin{cases} 1, & t \in \Omega = \{t \mid |\varepsilon(t)| \geq K_v\} \\ 0, & \text{elsewhere} \end{cases},$$

then (5.10) of Lemma 5.1 holds for all t if $\varepsilon(t)$ is replaced by $1_\Omega(t)\ \varepsilon(t)$. Furthermore, it follows from (B.21), (B.27), (B.26), and (B.18) that

$$\int_{T_{j-1}^i}^{T_{j+1}^i} |1_\Omega(s)\ \varepsilon(s)|\ ds \geq \int_{T_{j-1}^i}^{T_{j+1}^i} |\varepsilon(s)|\ ds - \left(T_{j+1}^i - T_{j-1}^i\right) K_v \geq$$

$$\geq \int_{T_{j-1}^i}^{T_{j+1}^i} |\varepsilon(s)|\ ds - 2\Delta T \cdot K_v \geq \int_{T_{j-1}^i}^{T_{j+1}^i} |\varepsilon(s)|\ ds - 2K_\Delta \ln N \cdot K_v \geq$$

$$\geq \int_{T_{j-1}^i}^{T_{j+1}^i} |\varepsilon(s)|\ ds - \frac{1}{2} \cdot \frac{N^{K_1(c_M + \rho K_T) + 4}}{4K\left(1 + \frac{K_5}{a}\right) K_\Delta \ln N \cdot N^{K_1 \rho K_T}} \geq$$

$$\geq \frac{1}{2} \int_{T_{j-1}^i}^{T_{j+1}^i} |\varepsilon(s)|\ ds \qquad \text{for N sufficiently large.}$$

It is then easy to see that (B.30) still holds if $\varepsilon(t)$ is replaced by $\varepsilon(t) \cdot 1_\Omega(t)$ in the derivation.

(ii) Lemma 5.1 is used in the same way as above in Step 3 of the proof. Since the technique is similar, the above modifications can be used here too.

(iii) The modification might cause $\dot{\hat{\theta}}(t)$ to be zero sometimes. The estimate used for $\hat{\theta}(t)$ in the proof of Lemma B.4 is, however, still valid.

The conclusion is that Theorem 5.1 can be applied and the theorem is proven. □

The comments on the modification of the estimation algorithm in discrete time apply here too.

Another possibility to obtain bounded estimates is to project them into a bounded area. This idea is exploited in the following theorem.

THEOREM 5.4 (CSA-algorithm with projection)

Consider the plant (5.1) controlled by the CSA-algorithm, modified in the following way:

$$\begin{cases} \dot{\hat{b}}_0(t) = \left[\dfrac{\overline{u}(t)}{P_1} + \hat{\theta}^T(t)\,\overline{\varphi}(t)\right]\dfrac{\varepsilon(t)}{r(t)} - \dfrac{\gamma}{r(t)}\,\hat{b}_0(t) \\ \dot{\hat{\theta}}(t) = \overline{\varphi}(t)\,\dfrac{\varepsilon(t)}{r(t)} - \dfrac{\gamma}{r(t)}\,\hat{\theta}(t) \end{cases} \quad ,\text{if} \quad \left\| \begin{pmatrix} \hat{b}_0(t) \\ \hat{\theta}(t) \end{pmatrix} \right\| \geq C, \tag{5.15}$$

where γ is a positive constant and the constant C satisfies

$$C > 2\sqrt{\frac{\max(1, b_0)}{\min(1, b_0)}} \cdot \left\| \begin{pmatrix} b_0 \\ \theta \end{pmatrix} \right\| , \tag{5.16}$$

where b_0 and θ are the true plant parameters. Assume that A1 - A4 are satisfied. Then the closed-loop system is L^∞-stable. □

Proof

Define

$$\psi^T = (b_0 \quad \sqrt{b_0}\,\theta^T)$$

$$\hat{\psi}^T(t) = (\hat{b}_0(t) \quad \sqrt{b_0}\,\hat{\theta}^T(t))$$

$$\tilde{\psi}^T(t) = (\tilde{b}_0(t) \quad \sqrt{b_0}\,\tilde{\theta}^T(t)).$$

It follows readily that

$$\min(1, b_0)\cdot(b_0^2 + |\theta|^2) \leq |\psi|^2 \leq \max(1, b_0)\cdot(b_0^2 + |\theta|^2) \qquad (5.17)$$

and analogously for $\hat{\psi}(t)$. When $|(\hat{b}_0(t) \quad \hat{\theta}^T(t))| \geq C$, it follows from (5.16) that, for some $0 < \mu < 1/2$,

$$|\hat{\psi}(t)|^2 \geq \min(1, b_0)\cdot(\hat{b}_0^2(t) + |\hat{\theta}(t)|^2) > \min(1, b_0)\cdot C^2 \geq$$

$$\geq \frac{1}{\mu^2} \max(1, b_0)\cdot(b_0^2 + |\theta|^2) \geq \frac{1}{\mu^2} |\psi|^2.$$

This implies that

$$|\psi| \leq \mu\, |\hat{\psi}(t)| \leq \mu\, (|\tilde{\psi}(t)| + |\psi|)$$

and so

$$|\psi| \leq \frac{\mu}{1-\mu} |\tilde{\psi}(t)| \quad \text{when (5.15) is used.}$$

Use this estimate of $|\psi|$ to get

$$|\tilde{\psi}(t)|^2 = \tilde{\psi}^T(t)(\hat{\psi}(t) - \psi) \leq \tilde{\psi}^T(t)\, \hat{\psi}(t) + |\tilde{\psi}(t)|\cdot|\psi| \leq$$

$$\leq \tilde{\psi}^T(t)\, \hat{\psi}(t) + \frac{\mu}{1-\mu} |\tilde{\psi}(t)|^2,$$

which implies

$$\tilde{\psi}^T(t)\, \hat{\psi}(t) \geq \frac{1-2\mu}{1-\mu} |\tilde{\psi}(t)|^2 \quad \text{when (5.15) is used.}$$

Lemma 5.1 says that without modification,

$$\frac{d}{dt}(|\tilde{\psi}(t)|^2) \leq -\frac{\varepsilon^2(t)}{r(t)} + \frac{K_v^2}{r(t)},$$

since the noise is uniformly bounded. Now, when the modification (5.15) is used, we have

$$\frac{d}{dt}(|\tilde{\psi}(t)|^2) = 2\,[\tilde{b}_0(t)\, \dot{\tilde{b}}_0(t) + b_0\, \tilde{\theta}^T(t)\, \dot{\tilde{\theta}}(t)] =$$

$$= 2\left[\tilde{b}_0(t)\left(\frac{\overline{u(t)}}{P_1} + \hat{\theta}^T(t)\, \overline{\varphi}(t)\right)\frac{\varepsilon(t)}{r(t)} - \frac{\gamma}{r(t)}\, \tilde{b}_0(t)\, \hat{b}_0(t) + \right.$$

$$+ b_0\, \tilde{\theta}^T(t)\, \bar{\varphi}(t)\, \frac{\varepsilon(t)}{r(t)} - \frac{\gamma}{r(t)}\, b_0\, \tilde{\theta}^T(t)\, \hat{\theta}(t)\Big] =$$

$$= 2\, \frac{\varepsilon(t)}{r(t)} \left(\frac{AR}{P}\, \bar{v}(t) - \varepsilon(t)\right) - 2\, \frac{\gamma}{r(t)} \left(\tilde{b}_0(t)\, \hat{b}_0(t) + b_0\, \tilde{\theta}^T(t)\, \hat{\theta}(t)\right) \leq$$

$$\leq - \frac{\varepsilon^2(t)}{r(t)} + \frac{K_v^2}{r(t)} - 2\, \frac{\gamma}{r(t)}\, \tilde{\psi}^T(t)\, \hat{\psi}(t) \leq$$

$$\leq - \frac{\varepsilon^2(t)}{r(t)} + \frac{K_v^2}{r(t)} - 2\, \frac{\gamma}{r(t)}\, \frac{1-2\mu}{1-\mu}\, |\tilde{\psi}(t)|^2. \qquad (5.18)$$

Two things follow from this result. Firstly, it is obvious that Lemma 5.1 holds even if the modification is used. Secondly, it follows from (5.17) that if

$$|\tilde{\psi}(t)| \geq |\psi| + C\sqrt{\max(1, b_0)}$$

then

$$\left\| \begin{pmatrix} \hat{b}_0(t) \\ \hat{\theta}(t) \end{pmatrix} \right\| \geq \frac{1}{\sqrt{\max(1, b_0)}} \cdot |\hat{\psi}(t)| \geq \frac{1}{\sqrt{\max(1, b_0)}} (|\tilde{\psi}(t)| - |\psi|) \geq C$$

and so the modification is used. This fact together with (5.15) implies that

$$|\tilde{\psi}(t)| \leq \max \left(|\psi| + C\sqrt{\max(1, b_0)},\; K_v \sqrt{\frac{1-\mu}{2\gamma(1-2\mu)}} \right)$$

which means that the parameter estimates are bounded.

To apply Theorem 5.1, it now only remains to modify the proof of Lemma B.4. It is easy to see that a constant is added to $|\bar{\varphi}(s)|\cdot|\varepsilon(s)|$ in the integrands in (B.47) when the projection is used. This does not influence the estimate (B.48). Equation (B.49) is still true if a constant is added to

$$\int_{t-T}^{t} |\varepsilon(s)|\, ds.$$

This does not influence the arguments in the proof of Theorem 5.1. This concludes the proof. □

5.3. Convergence in the disturbance-free case

Stability conditions are crucial in the convergence analysis of adaptive schemes. For example, convergence of the output error in the absence of noise could not readily be solved for continuous time systems, except for the case with pole excess equal to one or two. Compare with the discussion in the beginning of this chapter and in Chapter 3.

The results of the preceeding section prove the boundedness of the closed-loop signals. It thus follows that the output error converges to zero.

THEOREM 5.5 (CSA-algorithm without noise)

Consider the plant (5.1) with no noise, i.e. $v(t) = 0$, controlled by the CSA-algorithm. Assume that assumptions A1 - A4 are satisfied and that the command input $u^M(t)$ is uniformly bounded. The output error then converges to zero, i.e.

$$y(t) - y^M(t) \to 0, \quad t \to \infty. \qquad \square$$

Proof

Lemma 5.1 gives $(v(t) = 0)$

$$\int_0^\infty \frac{\varepsilon^2(t)}{r(t)} \, dt < \infty.$$

But $|\overline{\varphi}(t)|$ is bounded from Theorem 5.2 and $r(t)$ is therefore also bounded. Hence,

$$\int_0^\infty \varepsilon^2(t) \, dt < \infty. \tag{5.19}$$

This does not, however, imply that $\varepsilon(t)$ tends to zero. A bound on the derivative of $\varepsilon^2(t)$ is necessary for $\varepsilon(t)$ to converge to zero. It follows from (5.4) and (5.6 d,e,f) that

$$\varepsilon(t) = - \tilde{b}_0(t)\left(\hat{\theta}(t) - \frac{P_1(0)}{P_1(p)}\,\hat{\theta}(t)\right)^T \bar{\varphi}(t) - b_0\,\tilde{\theta}^T(t)\,\bar{\varphi}(t).$$

Thus, $\varepsilon(t)$ is bounded, because the parameter estimates and $|\bar{\varphi}(t)|$ are bounded. Define

$$H(p) = 1 - \frac{P_1(0)}{P_1(p)}$$

and differentiate the expression for $\varepsilon(t)$ to get

$$\dot{\varepsilon}(t) = - \left[\dot{\tilde{b}}_0(t)\left(H(p)\,\hat{\theta}(t)\right)^T \bar{\varphi}(t) + \tilde{b}_0(t)\left(H(p)\,\dot{\hat{\theta}}(t)\right)^T \bar{\varphi}(t) + \right.$$

$$\left. + \tilde{b}_0(t)\left(H(p)\,\hat{\theta}(t)\right)^T \dot{\bar{\varphi}}(t) + b_0\,\dot{\tilde{\theta}}^T(t)\,\bar{\varphi}(t) + b_0\,\tilde{\theta}^T(t)\,\dot{\bar{\varphi}}(t)\right] =$$

$$= - \left[\left(H(p)\,\hat{\theta}(t)\right)^T \bar{\varphi}(t)\,\frac{\varepsilon(t)}{r(t)}\left(H(p)\,\hat{\theta}(t)\right)^T \bar{\varphi}(t) + \right.$$

$$+ \tilde{b}_0(t)\left[H(p)\left(\bar{\varphi}(t)\,\frac{\varepsilon(t)}{r(t)}\right)\right]^T \bar{\varphi}(t) + \tilde{b}_0(t)\left(H(p)\,\hat{\theta}(t)\right)^T \dot{\bar{\varphi}}(t) +$$

$$\left. + b_0\,\bar{\varphi}^T(t)\,\frac{\varepsilon(t)}{r(t)}\,\bar{\varphi}(t) + b_0\,\tilde{\theta}^T(t)\,\dot{\bar{\varphi}}(t)\right].$$

The parameter estimates and $|\bar{\varphi}(t)|$ are bounded. Also, $\varepsilon(t)$ is bounded as was seen above. Furthermore, $H(p)$ is asymptotically stable and $r(t)$ is bounded from below by r_{min} as shown in the proof of Lemma B.3, Appendix B. Finally $|\dot{\bar{\varphi}}(t)|$ is bounded from the proof of Lemma B.2. It is thus possible to conclude that $\dot{\varepsilon}(t)$ is bounded. Hence,

$$\frac{d}{dt}\,[\varepsilon^2(t)] = 2\varepsilon(t)\,\dot{\varepsilon}(t)$$

is bounded. It then follows from (5.19) that

$$\varepsilon(t) \to 0, \quad t \to \infty.$$

In the same way as in Lemma B.4 (Appendix B), we have

$$\hat{e}_f(t) = \hat{b}_0(t)\left(G(p)\,\frac{\bar{\varphi}^T(t)\,\varepsilon(t)}{r(t)}\right)\bar{\varphi}(t),$$

where $G(p)$ is a strictly proper, asymptotically stable transfer operator. Since $|\hat{b}_0(t)|$ and $|\bar{\varphi}(t)|$ are bounded and $r(t) \geq r_{min}\ \forall\ t$, it thus follows that

$$\hat{e}_f(t) \to 0, \quad t \to \infty .$$

This implies that

$$e_f(t) = \varepsilon(t) + \hat{e}_f(t) \to 0, \quad t \to \infty .$$

Hence

$$y(t) - y^M(t) = e(t) = \frac{P(p)}{Q(p)} e_f(t) \to 0, \quad t \to \infty$$

because Q(p) is asymptotically stable and P(p)/Q(p) is proper. □

The output error thus converges to zero for the general algorithm defined in Chapter 3, provided that the estimation scheme and control law are chosen as for the CSA-algorithm. The output error will also converge to zero if the estimator is chosen as in the corollary or remark of Theorem 5.1.

In particular, convergence of the output error is assured for earlier propsed MRAS by Monopoli (1974) and Narendra/Valavani (1977) if some minor modifications of the algorithms are made. Firstly, the signals should be filtered by the transfer function Q/TA^M. In fact, this modification seems to improve the properties of the algorithms, cf. Example 4.1. Secondly, the parameter adjustment should have r(t) (or $|\overline{\varphi}(t)|^2$) in the denominator. Finally, the control law should be chosen as in (5.6f). It should also be noted that the same conclusions can be made for the algorithms by Bênêjean (1977) and Feuer/Morse (1977) and the new algorithm proposed in Section 3.3.

As in the discrete time case, it is possible to go one step further and investigate conditions for the convergence of the parameter estimates. It is then necessary to assume that the number of parameters is chosen correctly. Note that for the above results to hold, this was not required. The convergence of parameter estimates has been examined by others, e.g. Caroll/Lindorff (1973), Lüders/Narendra (1973),

Kudva/Narendra (1973), Morgan/Narendra (1977). The well-known conditions on the frequency contents of the input signal are introduced to assure convergence of parameter estimates. The problem will be left with these remarks.

References

Albert A E, Gardner L A (1967): *Stochastic Approximation and Nonlinear Regression*, The MIT Press, Cambridge, Mass.

Åström K J (1970): *Introduction to Stochastic Control Theory*, Academic Press, New York.

Åström K J (1976): *Reglerteori* (in Swedish), Almqvist & Wiksell (2nd edition), Stockholm.

Åström K J (1979): New implicit adaptive pole-placement algorithms for nonminimum phase systems. Report to appear, Dept of Automatic Control, Lund Institute of Technology, Lund, Sweden.

Åström K J, Bohlin T (1965): Numerical identification of linear dynamic systems from normal operating records. IFAC Symp on Theory of Self-adaptive Control Systems, Teddington, England.

Åström K J, Wittenmark B (1973): On self-tuning regulators. *Automatica* 9, 185-199.

Åström K J, Wittenmark B (1974): Analysis of a self-tuning regulator for nonminimum phase systems. Preprints of the IFAC Symp on Stochastic Control, Budapest, Hungary, 165-173.

Åström K J, Borisson U, Ljung L, Wittenmark B (1977): Theory and applications of self-tuning regulators. *Automatica* 13, 457-476.

Åström K J, Westerberg B, Wittenmark B (1978): Self-tuning controllers based on pole-placement design. CODEN: LUTFD2/(TFRT-3148)/1-52/(1978), Dept of Automatic Control, Lund Institute of Technology, Lund, Sweden.

Bénéjean R (1977): La commande adaptive à modèle de référence évolutif. Université Scientifique et Médicale de Grenoble, France.

Borisson U (1979): Self-tuning regulators for a class of multivariable systems. *Automatica* 15, 209-215.

Caroll R L, Lindorff P D (1973): An adaptive observer for single-input, single-output linear systems. *IEEE Trans Autom Control* AC-18, 496-499.

Clarke D W, Gawthrop P J (1975): Self-tuning controller. *Proc IEE* 122, 929-934.

Edmunds J M (1976): Digital adaptive pole shifting regulators. PhD dissertation, Control Systems Centre, University of Manchester, England.

Egardt B (1978): Stability of model reference adaptive and self-tuning regulators. CODEN: LUTFD2/(TFRT-1017)/1-163/(1978), Dept of Automatic Control, Lund Institute of Technology, Lund, Sweden.

Feuer A, Morse A S (1977): Adaptive control of single-input, single--output linear systems. Proc of the 1977 IEEE Conf on Decision and Control, New Orleans, USA, 1030-1035.

Feuer A, Morse A S (1978): Local stability of parameter-adaptive control systems. John Hopkin Conf on Information Science and Systems.

Feuer A, Barmish B R, Morse A S (1978): An unstable dynamical system associated with model reference adaptive control. *IEEE Trans Autom Control* AC-23, 499-500.

Gawthrop P J (1977): Some interpretations of the self-tuning controller. *Proc IEE* 124, 889-894.

Gawthrop P J (1978): On the stability and convergence of self-tuning algorithms. Report 1259/78, Dept of Engineering Science, University of Oxford.

Gilbart J W, Monopoli R V, Price C F (1970): Improved convergence and increased flexibility in the design of model reference adaptive control systems. Proc of the IEEE Symp on Adaptive Processes, Univ of Texas, Austin, USA.

Goodwin G C, Ramadge P J, Caines P E (1978a): Discrete time multivariable adaptive control. Div of Applied Sciences, Harvard University.

Goodwin G C, Ramadge P J, Caines P E (1978b): Discrete time stochastic adaptive control. Div of Applied Sciences, Harvard University.

Ionescu T, Monopoli R V (1977): Discrete model reference adaptive control with an augmented error signal. *Automatica* 13, 507-517.

Kalman R E (1958): Design of a self-optimizing control system. *Trans ASME* 80, 468-478.

Kudva P, Narendra K S (1973): Synthesis of an adaptive observer using Lyapunovs direct method. *Int J Control* 18, 1201-1210.

Kudva P, Narendra K S (1974): An identification procedure for discrete multivariable systems. *IEEE Trans Autom Control* AC-19, 549-552.

Landau I D (1974): A survey of model reference adaptive techniques - theory and applications. *Automatica* 10, 353-379.

Landau I D, Bêthoux G (1975): Algorithms for discrete time model reference adaptive systems. Proc of the 6th IFAC World Congress, Boston, USA, paper 58.4.

Ljung L (1977a): On positive real transfer functions and the convergence of some recursive schemes. *IEEE Trans Autom Control* AC-22, 539-550.

Ljung L (1977b): Analysis of recursive stochastic algorithms. *IEEE Trans Autom Control* AC-22, 551-575.

Ljung L, Landau I D (1978): Model reference adaptive systems and self--tuning regulators - some connections. Preprints of the 7th IFAC World Congress, Helsinki, Finland, 1973-1980.

Ljung L, Wittenmark B (1974): Asymptotic properties of self-tuning regulators. Report TFRT-3071, Dept of Automatic Control, Lund Institute of Technology, Lund, Sweden.

Ljung L, Wittenmark B (1976): On a stabilizing property of adaptive regulators. IFAC Symp on Identification and System Parameter Estimation, Tbilisi, USSR.

Lüders G, Narendra K S (1973): An adaptive observer and identifier for a linear system. *IEEE Trans Autom Control* AC-18, 496-499.

Monopoli R V (1973): The Kalman-Yakubovich lemma in adaptive control system design. *IEEE Trans Autom Control* AC-18, 527-529.

Monopoli R V (1974): Model reference adaptive control with an augmented error signal. *IEEE Trans Autom Control* AC-19, 474-484.

Morgan A P, Narendra K S (1977): On the uniform asymptotic stability of certain linear nonautonomous differential equations. *SIAM J Control* 15, 5-24.

Morse A S (1979): Global stability of parameter-adaptive control systems. Dept of Engineering and Applied Science, Yale University.

Narendra K S, Valavani L S (1976): Stable adaptive observers and controllers. *Proc of the IEEE* 64, 1198-1208.

Narendra K S, Valavani L S (1977): Stable adaptive controller design, part I: Direct control. Proc of the IEEE Conf on Decision and Control, New Orleans, USA, 881-886.

Narendra K S, Valavani L S (1978): Direct and indirect adaptive control. Preprints of the 7th IFAC World Congress, Helsinki, Finland, 1981-1987.

Osburn P V, Whitaker H P, Kezer A (1966): New developments in the design of adaptive control systems. Inst of Aeronautical Sciences, paper 61-39.

Parks P C (1966): Lyapunov redesign of model reference adaptive control systems. *IEEE Trans Autom Control* AC-11, 362-367.

Peterka V (1970): Adaptive digital regulation of noisy systems. 2nd IFAC Symp on Identification and System Parameter Estimation, Prague, Czechoslovakia.

Wellstead P E, Prager D, Zanker P, Edmunds J M (1978): Self tuning pole/zero assignment regulators. Report 404, Control Systems Centre, University of Manchester, England.

Appendix A - Proof of Theorem 4.1

Theorem 4.1

Consider a plant, described by

$$A(q^{-1})y(t) = q^{-(k+1)}b_0B(q^{-1})u(t) + w(t) \tag{A.1}$$

or, alternatively,

$$e_f(t) = b_0q^{-(k+1)}\left[\frac{\overline{u}(t)}{P_1} + \theta^T\overline{\varphi}(t)\right] + \frac{R}{P}\,\overline{w}(t). \tag{A.2}$$

Here '$\overline{\ }$' denotes filtering by Q/TA^M and

$$\varphi^T(t) = \left[\frac{u(t-1)}{P},\ldots,\frac{u(t-n_u)}{P},\ \frac{y(t)}{P},\ldots,\frac{y(t-n_y+1)}{P},\ -\frac{TB^M}{P}\,u^M(t)\right], \tag{A.3}$$

where

$$\begin{aligned} n_u &= \max\,(m+k,\ n_{P_2}) \\ n_y &= \max\,(n+n_T-k,\ n). \end{aligned} \tag{A.4}$$

The plant is controlled by the DSA-algorithm with fixed observer polynomial, defined by

- estimation scheme:

$$\hat{b}_0(t) = \hat{b}_0(t-1) + \left[\frac{\overline{u}(t-k-1)}{P_1} + \hat{\theta}^T(t-1)\overline{\varphi}(t-k-1)\right]\frac{\varepsilon(t)}{r(t)} \tag{A.5a}$$

$$\hat{\theta}(t) = \hat{\theta}(t-1) + \beta_0\,\overline{\varphi}(t-k-1)\,\frac{\varepsilon(t)}{r(t)} \tag{A.5b}$$

$$\begin{aligned} r(t) = \lambda r(t-1) &+ \left[\frac{\overline{u}(t-k-1)}{P_1} + \hat{\theta}^T(t-1)\overline{\varphi}(t-k-1)\right]^2 + \\ &+ \beta_0^2\,|\overline{\varphi}(t-k-1)|^2 + \alpha;\quad 0 \leqslant \lambda < 1;\ \alpha \geqslant 0 \end{aligned} \tag{A.5c}$$

$$\varepsilon(t) = e_f(t) - \hat{e}_f(t|t-1) \tag{A.5d}$$

$$\hat{e}_f(t|t-1) = \hat{b}_0(t-1)\left[\frac{\overline{u}(t-k-1)}{P_1} + \hat{\theta}^T(t-1)\overline{\varphi}(t-k-1)\right] \tag{A.5e}$$

- control law:

$$\frac{\bar{u}(t)}{P_1} = - \hat{\theta}^T(t)\,\bar{\varphi}(t) \tag{A.5f}$$

Assume that A.1 - A.3 are fulfilled. Further assume that the parameter estimates are uniformly bounded and that $0 < \frac{b_0}{2} < \beta_0$. Then the closed loop system is L^∞-stable, i.e. if $w(t)$ and $u^M(t)$ are uniformly bounded, then $u(t)$ and $y(t)$ are also uniformly bounded.

Proof

A single realization will be considered throughout the proof. This means that constants appearing in the estimates will depend on initial conditions and realizations of $w(t)$ and $u^M(t)$. The boundedness of $|\bar{\varphi}(t)|$ will be proved by contradiction. Thus, assume that

$$\sup_{t \geq 0} |\bar{\varphi}(t)| > NM$$

for N and M arbitrarily large. This assumption will be contradicted for some N and M. Under the assumption, t_{NM} and t_M are well-defined if $N > 1$ and $M > |\bar{\varphi}(0)|$:

$$t_{NM} = \min \{t \,|\, |\bar{\varphi}(t)| \geq NM\}$$

$$t_M = \max \{t \,|\, t \leq t_{NM};\ \ |\bar{\varphi}(t)| \geq M;$$
$$|\bar{\varphi}(s)| < M \ \forall\, s \in [\max(0, t - [c_M \ln N]), t-1]\} .$$

Here $[t]$ denotes the integer part of t and c_M is defined below. A schematic picture of $|\bar{\varphi}(t)|$ in the interval $[t_M, t_{NM}]$ is seen in Fig. A.1.

The contradiction will be achieved by analysing the algorithm in detail in the interval $[t_M, t_{NM}]$. An outline of the proof is as follows. In Step 1 an increasing subsequence of $\{|\bar{\varphi}(t)|\}$, $\{|\bar{\varphi}(\tau_i)|\}_{i=1}^{N_\tau}$, is defined and a lower bound on N_τ is derived. In Step 2 an upper bound on $\tau_{N_\tau} - \tau_1$ is given. Finally, Step 3 derives an upper bound on N_τ. Combining the results of Steps 1 and 3 gives the contradiction and the boundedness of $|\bar{\varphi}(t)|$ is thereby proved. It is then easy to conclude the boundedness of $u(t)$ and $y(t)$.

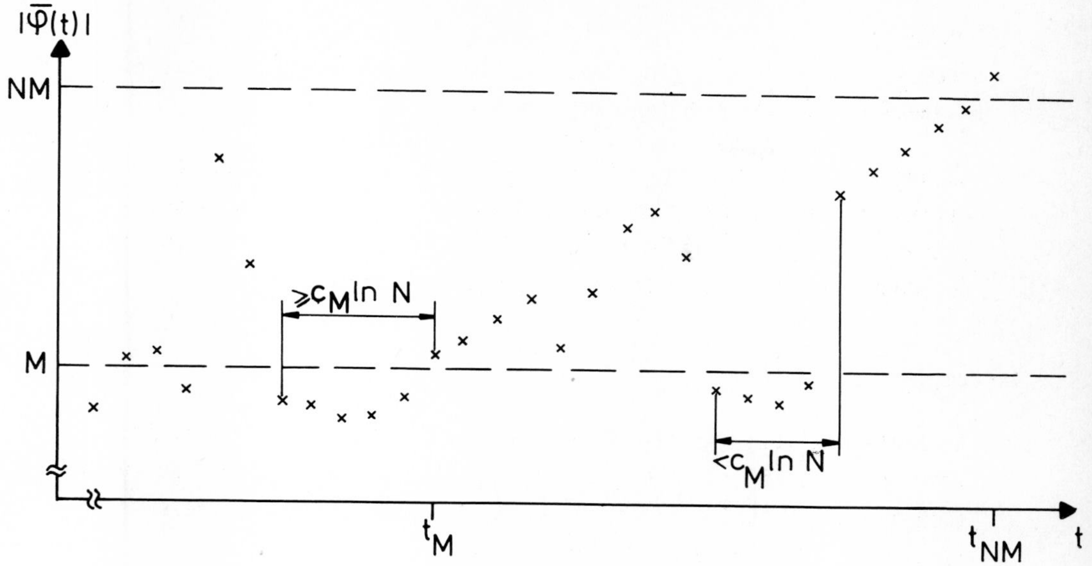

Figure A.1. The behaviour of $|\bar{\varphi}(t)|$ in the interval $[t_M, t_{NM}]$.

Some preliminary results are first given as separate lemmas. Proofs of these lemmas can be found at the end of the appendix.

Lemma A.1

Under the conditions of the theorem, there exist a positive constant K, a constant μ, $0 < \mu < 1$, and an asymptotically stable matrix F such that, for every $t \geqslant s+1$,

$$|\bar{\varphi}(t)| \leqslant \| F^{t-s} \| \cdot |\bar{\varphi}(s)| + (t-s)K\left(1 + \sup_{s \leqslant \tau < t} \sum_{\sigma=k+1}^{\tau+k+1} \mu^{\tau+k+1-\sigma} |e_f(\sigma)|\right). \qquad (A.6)$$

Lemma A.2

Under the conditions of the theorem, there exist positive constants K_1 and K_2 such that

$$|\bar{\varphi}(t+1)| \leqslant K_1 |\bar{\varphi}(t)| + K_2 \quad \forall\, t. \qquad (A.7)$$

Lemma A.3

Under the conditions of the theorem, there exist positive constants K_3 and K_4 such that, for $k \geq 1$,

$$|\hat{e}_f(t|t-1)| \leq \left(K_3 + \frac{K_4}{\min\limits_{t-2k-1 \leq s \leq t-k-2} |\bar{\varphi}(s)|}\right) \sup_{t-k \leq s \leq t-1} |\varepsilon(s)|. \tag{A.8}$$

Before we return to the proof, we will make the definition of t_M complete by defining

$$c_M = \max\left(\frac{1}{\ln(1/\mu)}, \frac{2}{\ln(1/\lambda)}\right) \tag{A.9}$$

where μ is from Lemma A.1. It is meant that $c_M = 1/\ln(1/\mu)$ if $\lambda=0$. Let $[s_1,s_2]$ be any interval between t_M and t_{NM} such that

$$|\bar{\varphi}(s)| < M \quad \forall \quad s_1 \leq s \leq s_2$$

$$|\bar{\varphi}(s_2+1)| \geq M.$$

Assuming $\min\limits_{s_1 \leq s \leq s_2} |\bar{\varphi}(s)|$ is attained for $s = s_0$, Lemma A.2 gives

$$M \leq |\bar{\varphi}(s_2+1)| \leq K_1^{s_2-s_0+1} |\bar{\varphi}(s_0)| + \left(K_1^{s_2-s_0} + K_1^{s_2-s_0-1} + \ldots + 1\right) K_2 \leq$$

$$\leq K_1^{s_2-s_0+1}\left(|\bar{\varphi}(s_0)| + \frac{K_2}{K_1 - 1}\right),$$

where it has been assumed that $K_1 > 1$, which is no restriction. The definition of t_M then implies

$$|\bar{\varphi}(s_0)| \geq \frac{M}{K_1^{s_2-s_0+1}} - \frac{K_2}{K_1 - 1} \geq \frac{M}{K_1^{c_M \ln N}} - \frac{K_2}{K_1 - 1} = \frac{M}{N^{c_M \ln K_1}} - \frac{K_2}{K_1 - 1}$$

and so, since the interval $[s_1,s_2]$ is arbitrary, we have for large N

$$\min_{t_M \leq s \leq t_{NM}} |\bar{\varphi}(s)| \geq \frac{M}{N^{c_M \ln K_1}} - \frac{K_2}{K_1 - 1} \geq \frac{1}{2} N^3, \tag{A.10}$$

where M has been chosen as

$$M = N^p \triangleq N^{c_M \ln K_1 + 3}. \tag{A.11}$$

Step 1. Characterization of the sequence $\{\overline{\varphi}(\tau_i)\}$

Assume from now on that $t_M < t_{NM}$. This is true for large N as seen from (A.7). Define the sequence $\{\tau_i\}_{i=1}^{N_\tau}$ recursively from

$$\begin{cases} \tau_1 = t_M \\ \tau_{i+1} = \min \{t \mid \tau_i + n_\tau \leq t < t_{NM},\ |\overline{\varphi}(t)| \geq \max_{t_M \leq s \leq t} |\overline{\varphi}(s)|\}, \end{cases}$$

where n_τ will be defined below. It is clear that the sequence is nondecreasing. An illustration of the definition is given in Fig. A.2, which shows the same realization as in Fig. A.1.

Define $N_F(x)$ to be the smallest integer that satisfies

$$\| F^i \| \leq \frac{1}{x} \quad \forall \quad i \geq N_F(x) \qquad (x > 0), \tag{A.12}$$

where F is defined in Lemma A.1. This is possible, because F is asymptotically stable. Also notice that from (A.2),(A.5f) and the boundedness of the estimates and the noise it follows that

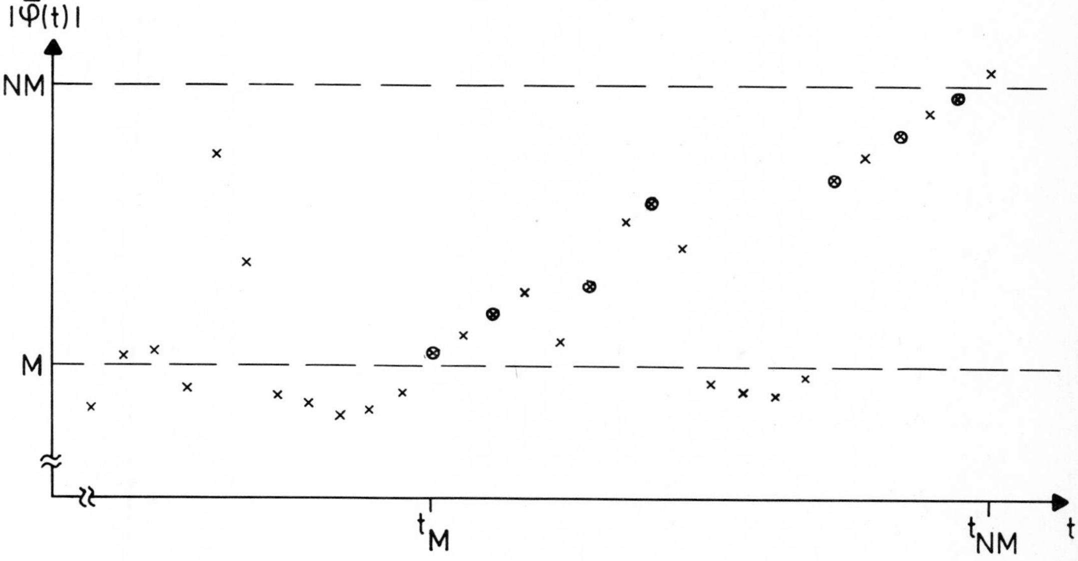

Figure A.2. The definition of $\{\tau_i\}$. The members of the sequence are marked with a ring. It is assumed that $n_\tau = 2$.

$$|e_f(t+k+1)| \leq K_e|\bar{\varphi}(t)| + K_v \tag{A.13}$$

for some constants K_e and K_v. Now choose n_τ as an integer which satisfies the following three conditions:

$$\begin{aligned}
&\text{(i)} \quad n_\tau \geq N_F(4) \\
&\text{(ii)} \quad n_\tau \geq k \\
&\text{(iii)} \quad n_\tau \mu^{n_\tau - k} \leq \frac{1-\mu}{8K(K_e+1)} \,.
\end{aligned} \tag{A.14}$$

Choose N so that

$$M \geq \max\left(\frac{K_2}{K_1-1}, K_2\right)$$

with K_1 and K_2 from Lemma A.2; it is assumed that $K_1 > 1$, which is no restriction. This can of course be achieved with an N large enough. Conditions like this one on N and M will appear several times in the sequel. It is then important to check that the constants appearing in these conditions do not depend on the interval under consideration and consequently on N and M themselves. This will however not be pointed out every time it appears.

If N is chosen as above, Lemma A.2 and the definition of $\{\tau_i\}$ give

$$\begin{aligned}
|\bar{\varphi}(\tau_{i+1})| &\leq K_1|\bar{\varphi}(\tau_{i+1}-1)| + K_2 \leq K_1 \sup_{\tau_i \leq t \leq \tau_i + n_\tau} |\bar{\varphi}(t)| + K_2 \leq \\
&\leq K_1^{n_\tau+1} |\bar{\varphi}(\tau_i)| + (K_1^{n_\tau} + K_1^{n_\tau - 1} + \ldots + 1)\, K_2 \leq \\
&\leq K_1^{n_\tau+1}\left(|\bar{\varphi}(\tau_i)| + \frac{K_2}{K_1-1}\right) \leq 2K_1^{n_\tau+1} |\bar{\varphi}(\tau_i)|.
\end{aligned}$$

It follows in the same way that

$$|\bar{\varphi}(t_{NM})| \leq 2K_1^{n_\tau+1} |\bar{\varphi}(\tau_{N_\tau})|$$

and so, combining these inequalities,

$$NM \leq |\overline{\varphi}(t_{NM})| \leq 2K_1^{n_\tau+1} |\overline{\varphi}(\tau_{N_\tau})| \leq \ldots \leq 2^{N_\tau} K_1^{N_\tau(n_\tau+1)} |\overline{\varphi}(\tau_1)| \leq$$

$$\leq 2^{N_\tau} K_1^{N_\tau(n_\tau+1)} (K_1 |\overline{\varphi}(\tau_1 - 1)| + K_2) \leq 2^{N_\tau} K_1^{N_\tau(n_\tau+1)} (K_1 M + K_2) \leq$$

$$\leq 2 \cdot 2^{N_\tau} K_1^{N_\tau(n_\tau+1)+1} M,$$

where the condition on M above has been used in the last step. The conclusion is thus that

$$N_\tau \geq \frac{\ln (N/2K_1)}{\ln 2 + \ln K_1 \cdot (n_\tau+1)} . \tag{A.15}$$

This is a lower bound on N_τ, which will be used later on. The first step of the proof is concluded.

Step 2. Derivation of an upper bound on $\tau_{N_\tau} - \tau_1$

Define intervals

$$I_i = [\tau_{i-1}, \tau_{i+1}], \quad i = 2, 4, \ldots, 2N_I$$

where the number of intervals N_I satisfies

$$N_I = \begin{cases} \frac{1}{2}(N_\tau - 1), & N_\tau \text{ odd.} \\ \frac{1}{2}(N_\tau - 2), & N_\tau \text{ even.} \end{cases} \tag{A.16}$$

and can be assumed positive from (A.15). Define the sequence $\{T_j^i\}_{j=0}^{N_T^i}$ inside the interval I_i (where i is arbitrary) through

$$\begin{cases} T_0^i = \tau_{i-1} \\ T_j^i = \min \{t | t \geq T_{j-1}^i + n_T, \ |\overline{\varphi}(t)| \geq M\}, \ j = 1, \ldots, N_T^i \end{cases} \tag{A.17}$$

where N_T^i satisfies

$$\tau_{i+1} - n_T < T_{N_T^i}^i \leq \tau_{i+1} \tag{A.18}$$

The left inequality follows because $|\overline{\varphi}(\tau_{i+1})| \geq M$. The integer n_T is defined as

$$n_T = K_T \ln N, \tag{A.19}$$

where

$$K_T = \max\left(\frac{2}{\ln[1/r(F)]}, \frac{2}{\ln(1/\mu)}\right). \tag{A.20}$$

Here r(F) is the spectral radius of the matrix F in Lemma A.1.

Denote by ΔT the maximal distance between any two successive members of the sequence $\{T_j^i\}$. Then it follows from (A.17) and the definition of t_M (cf. Fig. A.1) that

$$\Delta T \lesssim n_T + c_M \ln N = (K_T + c_M) \ln N \triangleq K_\Delta \ln N, \tag{A.21}$$

where K_Δ is independent of N.

Define intervals

$$J_j^i = \left[T_{j-1}^i, T_{j+1}^i\right], \quad j = 1, 3, \ldots, 2N_J^i - 1,$$

where the number of intervals N_J^i satisfies

$$N_J^i = \begin{cases} \frac{1}{2}(N_T^i - 1), & N_T^i \text{ odd} \\ \frac{1}{2} N_T^i, & N_T^i \text{ even.} \end{cases} \tag{A.22}$$

The algorithm will be examined in detail in an interval J_j^i. Distinguish between two cases.

The case $N_T^i \geq 2$

It is seen from (A.22) that there is at least one interval J_j^i inside the interval I_i. Suppose that

$$\sup_{T_{j-1}^i \leq s < T_{j+1}^i} |\varepsilon(s+k+1)| < \frac{(1-\mu) M}{4K(K_3 + K_4 + 1)\Delta T} \tag{A.23}$$

with K_3 and K_4 from Lemma A.3. This assumption will be shown to lead to a contradiction. We will first conclude that $n_T \geq N_F(4N)$ as defined in (A.12). The matrix F in (A.12) is asymptotically stable, which implies that there is a constant K_F such that

$$\| F^i \| \leq K_F \cdot r(F)^i \quad \forall \quad i \geq i_F$$

for some integer i_F. Here r(F), the spectral radius of F, is less than one. If $N_F(4N) \to \infty$, $N \to \infty$, the definition of $N_F(x)$, (A.12), gives

$$\frac{1}{4N} < \left\| F^{N_F(4N)-1} \right\| \leq K_F \cdot r(F)^{(N_F(4N)-1)} ,$$

which implies that

$$N_F(4N) \leq \frac{\ln 4K_F + \ln N}{\ln [1/r(F)]} + 1 \leq \frac{2}{\ln [1/r(F)]} \ln N \leq n_T$$

for N sufficiently large.

On the other hand, if $N_F(4N)$ is uniformly bounded in N, then the above result is still true. It is therefore possible to use Lemma A.1 and the definitions of $N_F(4N)$ and ΔT to obtain:

$$|\bar{\varphi}(T^i_{j+1})| \leq \frac{|\bar{\varphi}(T^i_j)|}{4N} + K\Delta T \left(1 + \sup_{T^i_j \leq \tau < T^i_{j+1}} \sum_{\sigma=k+1}^{\tau+k+1} \mu^{\tau+k+1-\sigma} |e_f(\sigma)|\right).$$

Suppose the sup is attained for $\tau = t$. Then

$$|\bar{\varphi}(T^i_{j+1})| \leq \frac{|\bar{\varphi}(T^i_j)|}{4N} + K\Delta T \left(1 + \sum_{\sigma=k+1}^{t+k+1} \mu^{t+k+1-\sigma} |e_f(\sigma)|\right) \leq$$

$$\leq \frac{NM}{4N} + K\Delta T + K\Delta T \, \mu^{t-T^i_{j-1}-k+1} \sum_{\sigma=0}^{T^i_{j-1}+k-1} \mu^{T^i_{j-1}+k-1-\sigma} |e_f(\sigma+k+1)| +$$

$$+ K\Delta T \sum_{\sigma=T^i_{j-1}+k}^{t} \mu^{t-\sigma} |e_f(\sigma+k+1)| \triangleq \frac{M}{4} + K\Delta T + R_1 + R_2. \qquad \text{(A.24)}$$

The terms R_1 and R_2 will be considered separately.

First, it follows from (A.13) and the fact that $n_T \geq k$ that

$$R_1 \leq K\Delta T\, \mu^{n_T-k+1} \sum_{\sigma=0}^{T_{j-1}^i+k-1} \mu^{T_{j-1}^i+k-1-\sigma} (K_e|\bar{\varphi}(\sigma)| + K_v) \leq$$

$$\leq K\Delta T\, \mu^{n_T-k+1} \frac{1}{1-\mu} (K_e NM + K_v) \leq \frac{K}{1-\mu} (K_e+1)\Delta T\, \mu^{n_T-k+1}\, NM \leq$$

$$\leq \frac{K}{1-\mu} (K_e+1)\, \mu^{1-k}\, K_\Delta \ln N \cdot N^{-K_T \ln(1/\mu)} NM \leq \frac{M}{4},$$

where (A.21) and the definition of n_T, (A.19),(A.20), have also been used in the two last steps.

The term R_2 can be estimated using (A.5d) and Lemma A.3:

$$R_2 \leq K\Delta T \sum_{\sigma=T_{j-1}^i+k}^{t} \mu^{t-\sigma} (|\varepsilon(\sigma+k+1)| + |\hat{e}_f(\sigma+k+1|\sigma+k)|) \leq$$

$$\leq K\Delta T \sum_{\sigma=T_{j-1}^i+k}^{t} \mu^{t-\sigma} \left[|\varepsilon(\sigma+k+1)| + \left(K_3 + \frac{K_4}{\min_{\sigma-k\leq s\leq\sigma-1} |\bar{\varphi}(s)|}\right) \sup_{\sigma-k\leq s\leq\sigma-1} |\varepsilon(s+k+1)|\right] \leq$$

$$\leq K\Delta T \sum_{\sigma=T_{j-1}^i+k}^{t} \mu^{t-\sigma}(K_3 + K_4 + 1) \sup_{\sigma-k\leq s\leq\sigma} |\varepsilon(s+k+1)| \leq$$

$$\leq \frac{K}{1-\mu} (K_3 + K_4 + 1)\, \Delta T \sup_{T_{j-1}^i\leq s<T_{j+1}^i} |\varepsilon(s+k+1)| < \frac{M}{4},$$

according to the assumption (A.23). Here it has been used that

$$\min_{t_M\leq t\leq t_{NM}} |\bar{\varphi}(t)| \geq 1,$$

which follows from (A.10). Using the estimates of R_1 and R_2 in (A.24), the following is obtained:

$$|\bar{\varphi}(T_{j+1}^i)| < \frac{3}{4} M + K\Delta T \leq M$$

if

$$K\Delta T \leq \frac{M}{4} = \frac{N^P}{4} .$$

This condition is trivially satisfied for large N as seen from (A.21). We have thus arrived at a contradiction since $|\bar{\varphi}(T_{j+1}^i)| \geq M$ by construction. It is possible to conclude that

$$\sup_{T_{j-1}^i \leq s < T_{j+1}^i} |\varepsilon(s+k+1)| \geq \frac{(1-\mu)\ M}{4K(K_3 + K_4 + 1)\Delta T} . \tag{A.25}$$

This inequality is valid for all intervals J_j^i.

Define

$$V(t) = \tilde{b}_0^2(t) + \frac{b_0}{\beta_0} |\tilde{\theta}(t)|^2 \tag{A.26}$$

and suppose the supremum in (A.25) is obtained for s = t. Lemma 4.2 then gives

$$V(T_{j+1}^i+k) - V(T_{j-1}^i+k) \leq - c \sum_{s=T_{j-1}^i+k+1}^{T_{j+1}^i+k} \frac{\varepsilon^2(s)}{r(s)} + \frac{1}{c} \sum_{s=T_{j-1}^i+k+1}^{T_{j+1}^i+k} \frac{1}{r(s)} \left(\frac{R}{P}\bar{w}(s)\right)^2 \leq$$

$$\leq - c \frac{\varepsilon^2(t+k+1)}{r(t+k+1)} + \frac{K_v^2}{c} \sum_{s=T_{j-1}^i}^{T_{j+1}^i-1} \frac{1}{r(s+k+1)} ,$$

where K_v is the bound on the noise in (A.13). It follows from (A.5 c,f) and the boundedness of the estimates that, for $T_{j-1}^i \leq t < T_{j+1}^i$,

$$r(t+k+1) \leq r(k+1) + \frac{\alpha}{1-\lambda} + K_r \sum_{s=0}^{t} \lambda^{t-s} |\bar{\varphi}(s)|^2 \leq$$

$$\leq r(k+1) + \frac{\alpha}{1-\lambda} + \frac{K_r}{1-\lambda} (NM)^2 \leq \frac{2K_r}{1-\lambda} (NM)^2,$$

for some K_r if N is chosen sufficiently large. Furthermore, from (A.5c) and (A.10) a lower bound on r(t) can be obtained:

$$r(t+k+1) \geq \beta_0^2 |\bar{\varphi}(t)|^2 \geq \beta_0^2 \frac{1}{4} N^6. \tag{A.27}$$

If these two results are used above, the following inequality is obtained:

$$V(T^i_{j+1}+k) - V(T^i_{j-1}+k) \leq -\frac{c(1-\lambda)}{2K_r(NM)^2}\,\varepsilon^2(t+k+1) + \frac{2\Delta T\; K_v^2}{c\;\beta_0^2}\cdot\frac{4}{N^6}$$

and so, using (A.25), we have for N sufficiently large:

$$V(T^i_{j+1}+k) - V(T^i_{j-1}+k) \leq$$

$$\leq -\frac{c(1-\lambda)}{2K_r(NM)^2}\cdot\left(\frac{(1-\mu)\;M}{4K(K_3+K_4+1)\Delta T}\right)^2 + \frac{8\Delta T\;K_v^2}{c\;\beta_0^2\;N^6} \leq$$

$$\leq -\frac{c(1-\lambda)(1-\mu)^2}{N^2\Delta T^2\;2K_r[4K(K_3+K_4+1)]^2} + \frac{8\Delta T\;K_v^2}{c\;\beta_0^2\;N^6} \triangleq$$

$$\triangleq -\frac{c_1}{N^2\;\Delta T^2} + \frac{c_2\;\Delta T}{N^6}\,, \tag{A.28}$$

where c_1 and c_2 are independent of N.

Use the estimate of ΔT in (A.21) to obtain

$$V(T^i_{j+1}+k) - V(T^i_{j-1}+k) \leq -\frac{c_1}{N^2K_\Delta^2(\ln N)^2} + \frac{c_2K_\Delta\;\ln N}{N^6} \leq$$

$$\leq -\frac{1}{N^4}\left[\frac{c_1}{K_\Delta^2} - \frac{c_2K_\Delta\;\ln N}{N^2}\right] \leq -\frac{c_0}{N^4}$$

for N sufficiently large. Here c_0 is independent of N. This inequality holds for every interval J^i_j, i.e. N^i_J times. Thus,

$$V(T^i_{2N^i_J}+k) - V(T^i_0+k) \leq -c_0\,\frac{N^i_J}{N^4}.$$

But V is positive and bounded. If the bound is denoted by $\tilde{K}_v$, we have

$$N^i_J \leq \frac{\tilde{K}_v}{c_0}\cdot N^4. \tag{A.29}$$

The case $N_T^i < 2$

It is seen from (A.22) that in this case $N_J^i = 0$. Consequently, (A.29) is trivially satisfied.

The conclusion is thus that (A.29) is valid in every interval I_i, provided N is chosen large enough. The inequality (A.18) and (A.22) imply

$$\tau_{i+1} - T^i_{2N_J^i} = \left(\tau_{i+1} - T^i_{N_T^i}\right) + \left(T^i_{N_T^i} - T^i_{2N_J^i}\right) \leqslant n_T + \Delta T \leqslant 2\Delta T,$$

and so, by using (A.29),

$$\tau_{i+1} - \tau_{i-1} = \left(\tau_{i+1} - T^i_{2N_J^i}\right) + \left(T^i_{2N_J^i} - \tau_{i-1}\right) \leqslant$$

$$\leqslant 2\Delta T + 2N_J^i \Delta T \leqslant 2\Delta T\left(1 + \frac{\tilde{K}_v}{c_0} N^4\right) \leqslant \frac{4\tilde{K}_v}{c_0} \Delta T \cdot N^4 .$$

Summing for $i = 2, 4, \ldots, 2N_I$ gives

$$\tau_{2N_I+1} - \tau_1 \leqslant \frac{4\tilde{K}_v}{c_0} \Delta T \cdot N^4 \cdot N_I, \tag{A.30}$$

which ends Step 2 of the proof.

Step 3. Derivation of an upper bound on N_τ and the contradiction

Consider an interval I_i defined in Step 2. Suppose that

$$\sup_{\tau_{i+1}-2n_\tau \leqslant s < \tau_{i+1}} |\varepsilon(s+k+1)| < \frac{(1-\mu)|\overline{\varphi}(\tau_{i+1})|}{4Kn_\tau(K_3+K_4+1)} . \tag{A.31}$$

This will lead to a contradiction in the same way as in Step 2. Thus, analogously with (A.24) we have

$$|\overline{\varphi}(\tau_{i+1})| \leqslant \frac{|\overline{\varphi}(\tau_{i+1} - n_\tau)|}{4} + Kn_\tau + R_1 + R_2,$$

where

$$R_1 = Kn_\tau \mu^{t-\tau_{i+1}+2n_\tau-k+1} \sum_{\sigma=0}^{\tau_{i+1}-2n_\tau+k-1} \mu^{\tau_{i+1}-2n_\tau+k-1-\sigma} |e_f(\sigma+k+1)|$$

$$R_2 = Kn_\tau \sum_{\sigma=\tau_{i+1}-2n_\tau+k}^{t} \mu^{t-\sigma} |e_f(\sigma+k+1)|$$

and t is in the interval $[\tau_{i+1}-n_\tau, \tau_{i+1}-1]$. Notice that the property (A.14 i) of n_τ has been used.

Let [t] denote the integer part of t and estimate R_1 by using (A.13) and the inequality $K_v \leqslant M = N^p$, which is valid for N large enough:

$$R_1 \leqslant Kn_\tau \mu^{n_\tau-k+1}\Big[\mu^{\tau_{i+1}-2n_\tau+k-1-(t_M-[c_M \ln N]-1)} \cdot$$

$$\cdot \sum_{\sigma=0}^{t_M-[c_M \ln N]-1} \mu^{t_M-[c_M \ln N]-1-\sigma} |e_f(\sigma+k+1)| +$$

$$+ \sum_{\sigma=t_M-[c_M \ln N]}^{\tau_{i+1}-2n_\tau+k-1} \mu^{\tau_{i+1}-2n_\tau+k-1-\sigma} |e_f(\sigma+k+1)|\Big] \leqslant$$

$$\leqslant Kn_\tau \mu^{n_\tau-k+1} (K_e+1)\Big[\mu^{[c_M \ln N]+k} \frac{NM}{1-\mu} + \frac{|\overline{\varphi}(\tau_{i+1})|}{1-\mu}\Big],$$

where (A.14 ii) has been used in the last step. Now use (A.9) and (A.14 iii) to obtain

$$R_1 \leqslant Kn_\tau \mu^{n_\tau-k} (K_e+1)\Big[\frac{M}{1-\mu} + \frac{|\overline{\varphi}(\tau_{i+1})|}{1-\mu}\Big] \leqslant$$

$$\leqslant Kn_\tau \mu^{n_\tau-k} (K_e+1) \frac{2}{1-\mu} |\overline{\varphi}(\tau_{i+1})| \leqslant \frac{|\overline{\varphi}(\tau_{i+1})|}{4} .$$

The term R_2 is estimated as in Step 2 using the assumption (A.31):

$$R_2 \leqslant Kn_\tau \cdot \frac{K_3+K_4+1}{1-\mu} \sup_{\tau_{i+1}-2n_\tau \leqslant s < \tau_{i+1}} |\varepsilon(s+k+1)| < \frac{|\overline{\varphi}(\tau_{i+1})|}{4} .$$

Insert the estimates of R_1 and R_2 above, which gives

$$|\bar{\varphi}(\tau_{i+1})| < \frac{|\bar{\varphi}(\tau_{i+1} - n_\tau)|}{4} + Kn_\tau + \frac{|\bar{\varphi}(\tau_{i+1})|}{2} \leqslant |\bar{\varphi}(\tau_{i+1})|,$$

if

$$Kn_\tau \leqslant M = N^p,$$

which of course is satisfied for large N. This gives a contradiction and consequently the assumption (A.31) is false. Hence,

$$\sup_{\tau_{i+1}-2n_\tau \leqslant s < \tau_{i+1}} |\varepsilon(s+k+1)| \geqslant \frac{(1-\mu)|\bar{\varphi}(\tau_{i+1})|}{4Kn_\tau(K_3+K_4+1)} \tag{A.32}$$

in every interval I_i.

In the same way as in Step 2, (A.5 c,f) and the boundedness of the estimates imply that, for $\tau_{i-1} \leqslant s \leqslant \tau_{i+1}$,

$$r(s+k+1) \leqslant r(k+1) + \frac{\alpha}{1-\lambda} + K_r \sum_{\sigma=0}^{s} \lambda^{s-\sigma} |\bar{\varphi}(\sigma)|^2 = r(k+1) + \frac{\alpha}{1-\lambda} +$$

$$+ K_r \lambda^{s-(t_M-[c_M \ln N]-1)} \sum_{\sigma=0}^{t_M-[c_M \ln N]-1} \lambda^{t_M-[c_M \ln N]-1-\sigma} |\bar{\varphi}(\sigma)|^2 +$$

$$+ K_r \sum_{\sigma=t_M-[c_M \ln N]}^{s} \lambda^{s-\sigma} |\bar{\varphi}(\sigma)|^2 \leqslant$$

$$\leqslant r(k+1) + \frac{\alpha}{1-\lambda} + K_r \lambda^{[c_M \ln N]+1} \frac{(NM)^2}{1-\lambda} + K_r \frac{|\bar{\varphi}(\tau_{i+1})|^2}{1-\lambda} \leqslant$$

$$\leqslant r(k+1) + \frac{\alpha}{1-\lambda} + \frac{2K_r}{1-\lambda} |\bar{\varphi}(\tau_{i+1})|^2 \leqslant \frac{3K_r}{1-\lambda} |\bar{\varphi}(\tau_{i+1})|^2, \tag{A.33}$$

for large N and (A.9) has been used in the second last step.

Now use Lemma 4.2 in the same way as in Step 2, which gives

$$V(\tau_{i+1}+k) - V(\tau_{i-1}+k) \leqslant - c \sum_{s=\tau_{i-1}}^{\tau_{i+1}-1} \frac{\varepsilon^2(s+k+1)}{r(s+k+1)} + \frac{K_v^2}{c} \sum_{s=\tau_{i-1}}^{\tau_{i+1}-1} \frac{1}{r(s+k+1)} \leqslant$$

$$\leqslant - c \frac{\varepsilon^2(t+k+1)}{r(t+k+1)} + \frac{K_v^2}{c} \cdot \sum_{s=\tau_{i-1}}^{\tau_{i+1}-1} \frac{1}{r(s+k+1)} ,$$

where the supremum in (A.32) is attained for $s = t$. Using (A.32), (A.33), and (A.27) we have for N large enough:

$$V(\tau_{i+1}+k) - V(\tau_{i-1}+k) \leqslant - c \frac{(1-\mu)^2(1-\lambda)}{[4Kn_\tau(K_3+K_4+1)]^2 3K_r} + \frac{4K_v^2}{c\beta_0^2} \cdot \frac{\tau_{i+1} - \tau_{i-1}}{N^6} \triangleq$$

$$\triangleq - c_3 + c_4 \cdot \frac{\tau_{i+1} - \tau_{i-1}}{N^6} ,$$

where c_3 and c_4 are independent of N. The inequality is valid for $i = 2, 4, \ldots, 2N_I$ and so

$$V(\tau_{2N_I+1}+k) - V(\tau_1+k) \leqslant - c_3 N_I + c_4 \frac{\tau_{2N_I+1} - \tau_1}{N^6} \leqslant$$

$$\leqslant - c_3 N_I + \frac{c_4}{N^6} \cdot \frac{4\tilde{K}_v}{c_0} \Delta T \cdot N^4 \cdot N_I = - N_I\left(c_3 - \frac{4c_4\tilde{K}_v}{c_0} \cdot \frac{\Delta T}{N^2}\right),$$

where (A.30) is used in the second last step. But as in Step 2 $V(t)$ is positive and bounded from above by $\tilde{K}_v$, so that

$$N_I \leqslant \frac{\tilde{K}_v}{\left|c_3 - \frac{4c_4\tilde{K}_v}{c_0} \cdot \frac{\Delta T}{N^2}\right|} \leqslant \frac{\tilde{K}_v}{c_3 - c_{3/2}} = \frac{2\tilde{K}_v}{c_3}$$

for N sufficiently large. This follows from (A.21). From (A.16) it then follows that

$$N_\tau \leqslant 2N_I+2 \leqslant \frac{4\tilde{K}_v}{c_3} + 2,$$

i.e. N_τ is bounded by a constant. This is in disagreement with the result of Step 1, (A.15). We have thus lead the existence of arbitrarily large $|\bar{\varphi}(t)|$ into contradiction and it is thus proved that $|\bar{\varphi}(t)|$ is uniformly bounded.

It remains only to conclude that $|\overline{\varphi}(t)|$ bounded implies u(t) and y(t) bounded. But since $Q(q^{-1})$ is asymptotically stable, $|\overline{\varphi}(t)|$ bounded implies that $|\varphi(t)|$ is also bounded. From (A.3) it immediately follows that u(t) and y(t) are bounded. The proof is thus complete.

□

Proof of Lemma A.1

It follows from Lemma 4.1 that

$$\overline{\varphi}(t+1) = F\overline{\varphi}(t) + \begin{pmatrix} \frac{1}{b_0} \cdot \frac{A}{P}\,\overline{e}(t+k+1) \\ 0 \\ \vdots \\ 0 \\ \frac{1}{P}\,\overline{e}(t+1) \\ 0 \\ \vdots \\ 0 \end{pmatrix} + g_1(t) \triangleq F\,\overline{\varphi}(t) + g_2(t) + g_1(t),$$

where F is asymptotically stable and $g_1(t)$ is a vector consisting of filtered u^M and w. The vector $g_1(t)$ is therefore bounded, by a constant K_1 say. Iterate the above equation to obtain

$$\overline{\varphi}(t) = F^{t-s}\,\overline{\varphi}(s) + \sum_{i=s+1}^{t} F^{t-i}\,g_2(i-1) + \sum_{i=s+1}^{t} F^{t-i}\,g_1(i-1).$$

Since F is asymptotically stable,

$$\sup_{t\geqslant 0} \|F^t\| \triangleq K_F < \infty.$$

Also note that

$$\overline{e}(t) = \frac{Q}{TA^M}\,e(t) = \frac{P}{TA^M}\,e_f(t)$$

which implies

$$g_2(t) = \begin{pmatrix} \frac{1}{b_0} \cdot \frac{A}{TA^M} e_f(t+k+1) \\ 0 \\ \vdots \\ 0 \\ \frac{1}{TA^M} e_f(t+1) \\ 0 \\ \vdots \\ 0 \end{pmatrix}$$

But both T and A^M are asymptotically stable polynomials, so that

$$|g_2(t)| \leq K_2 \left(1 + \sum_{s=k+1}^{t+k+1} \mu^{t+k+1-s} |e_f(s)|\right)$$

for some $K_2 > 0$ and $0 < \mu < 1$.

Use these inequalities above to get

$$|\bar{\varphi}(t)| \leq \| F^{t-s} \| \cdot |\bar{\varphi}(s)| +$$

$$+ K_F(t-s)\left[\sup_{s\leq\tau<t} K_2\left(1 + \sum_{\sigma=k+1}^{\tau+k+1} \mu^{\tau+k+1-\sigma} |e_f(\sigma)|\right) + K_1\right]$$

which gives (A.6) with the choice $K = K_F(K_1+K_2)$. □

<u>Proof of Lemma A.2</u>

The definition of $\varphi(t)$, (A.3), gives

$$\overline{\varphi}(t+1) = \left[\begin{array}{cccc|cccc|c} 0 & & & & & & & & \\ 1 & & & & & & & & \\ & \ddots & & & & & & & \\ & & 1 & 0 & & & & & \\ \hline & & & & 0 & & & & \\ & & & & 1 & & & & \\ & & & & & \ddots & & & \\ & & & & & & 1 & 0 & \\ \hline & & & & & & & & 0 \end{array}\right] \overline{\varphi}(t) + \left[\begin{array}{c} \dfrac{\overline{u}(t)}{P} \\ 0 \\ \vdots \\ 0 \\ \dfrac{\overline{y}(t+1)}{P} \\ 0 \\ \vdots \\ 0 \\ -\dfrac{TB^M}{P}\,\overline{u}^M(t+1) \end{array}\right] \tag{A.34}$$

It follows from (A.5 f) and the definition of P_2 that

$$\frac{\overline{u}(t)}{P} = (1 - P_2)\,\frac{\overline{u}(t)}{P} + \frac{\overline{u}(t)}{P_1} =$$

$$= - \left[\, p_{21} \dots p_{2n_{P_2}} \quad 0 \dots 0 \,\right] \overline{\varphi}(t) - \hat{\theta}^T(t)\,\overline{\varphi}(t), \tag{A.35}$$

where the fact $n_u \geq n_{P_2}$ from (A.4) has been used. The equation (A.1) gives

$$\frac{\overline{y}(t+1)}{P} = - a_1 \frac{\overline{y}(t)}{P} - \dots - a_n \frac{\overline{y}(t-n+1)}{P} +$$

$$+ b_0\left(\frac{\overline{u}(t-k)}{P} + b_1 \frac{\overline{u}(t-k-1)}{P} + \dots + b_m \frac{\overline{u}(t-m-k)}{P}\right) + \frac{\overline{w}(t+1)}{P}$$

which, if $k > 0$, can be written

$$\frac{\overline{y}(t+1)}{P} = \left[\, 0 \dots 0 \;\; b_0 \;\; b_0 b_1 \dots b_0 b_m \;\; 0 \dots 0 \;\; -a_1 \dots -a_n \;\; 0 \dots 0 \,\right] \overline{\varphi}(t) +$$

$$+ \frac{\overline{w}(t+1)}{P}\,. \tag{A.36}$$

On the other hand, if $k = 0$ (A.35) can be used to get

$$\frac{\overline{y(t+1)}}{P} = \left[b_0 b_1 \ldots b_0 b_m \quad 0 \ldots 0 \quad -a_1 \ldots -a_n \quad 0 \ldots 0\right] \overline{\varphi}(t) -$$

$$- b_0 \left[p_{21} \ldots p_{2n_{P_2}} \quad 0 \ldots 0\right] \overline{\varphi}(t) - b_0 \hat{\theta}^T(t)\, \overline{\varphi}(t) +$$

$$+ \frac{\overline{w(t+1)}}{P} . \tag{A.37}$$

If (A.35) and (A.36) or (A.37) are inserted into (A.34), the following is obtained:

$$\overline{\varphi}(t+1) = A(t)\, \overline{\varphi}(t) + b(t),$$

where $A(t)$ is a matrix with bounded elements because the parameter estimates are assumed to be bounded. Also, the vector $b(t)$ is bounded because its components are outputs of asymptotically stable filters with inputs $w(t)$ and $u^M(t)$, which are bounded. The lemma is thus proven with $K_1 = \sup_t \| A(t) \|$ and $K_2 = \sup_t |b(t)|$. □

Proof of Lemma A.3

It follows from (A.5 e,f,b) that

$$|\hat{e}_f(t|t-1)| \leq |\hat{b}_0(t-1)| \left| [\hat{\theta}^T(t-1) - \hat{\theta}^T(t-k-1)]\, \overline{\varphi}(t-k-1) \right| =$$

$$= |\hat{b}_0(t-1)| \cdot \beta_0 \left| \overline{\varphi}^T(t-k-2) \frac{\varepsilon(t-1)}{r(t-1)} + \ldots + \overline{\varphi}^T(t-2k-1) \frac{\varepsilon(t-k)}{r(t-k)} \right| \cdot |\overline{\varphi}(t-k-1)| \leq$$

$$\leq |\hat{b}_0(t-1)| \cdot \frac{1}{\beta_0} \left(\frac{1}{|\overline{\varphi}(t-k-2)|} + \ldots + \frac{1}{|\overline{\varphi}(t-2k-1)|} \right) |\overline{\varphi}(t-k-1)| \cdot \sup_{t-k \leq s \leq t-1} |\varepsilon(s)|,$$

where (A.5 c) is used in the last step. From Lemma A.2 it follows that there are constants K_3' and K_4', such that

$$|\overline{\varphi}(t-k-1)| \leq K_3' \, |\overline{\varphi}(t-k-1-i)| + K_4', \quad i = 1, \ldots, k .$$

Insert this into the inequality above and use the boundedness of $\hat{b}_0(t)$ to obtain

$$|\hat{e}_f(t|t-1)| \leqslant |\hat{b}_0(t-1)| \cdot \frac{k}{\beta_0}\left(K_3' + \frac{K_4'}{\min\limits_{t-2k-1\leqslant s\leqslant t-k-2} |\overline{\varphi}(s)|}\right) \sup_{t-k\leqslant s\leqslant t-1} |\varepsilon(s)| \leqslant$$

$$\leqslant \left(K_3 + \frac{K_4}{\min\limits_{t-2k-1\leqslant s\leqslant t-k-2} |\overline{\varphi}(s)|}\right) \sup_{t-k\leqslant s\leqslant t-1} |\varepsilon(s)|$$

and the lemma is proven. □

APPENDIX B - PROOF OF THEOREM 5.1

Theorem 5.1

Consider a plant, described by

$$y(t) = \frac{b_0 \, B(p)}{A(p)} u(t) + v(t) \tag{B.1}$$

or, alternatively,

$$e_f(t) = b_0 \left[\frac{\overline{u}(t)}{P_1} + \theta^T \, \overline{\varphi}(t)\right] + \frac{AR}{P} \overline{v}(t). \tag{B.2}$$

Here '$\overline{}$' denotes filtering by Q/TA^M and

$$\varphi^T(t) = \left[\frac{p^{m+n_T-1}}{P} u(t),\ldots, \frac{u(t)}{P}, \; \frac{p^{n-1}}{P} y(t),\ldots, \frac{y(t)}{P}, \; - \frac{TB^M}{P} u^M(t)\right]. \tag{B.3}$$

The plant is controlled by the CSA-algorithm, defined by

- estimation algorithm:

$$\begin{cases}
\dot{\tilde{b}}_0(t) = \left(\dfrac{\overline{u}(t)}{P_1} + \hat{\theta}^T(t) \, \overline{\varphi}(t)\right) \dfrac{\varepsilon(t)}{r(t)} & \text{(B.4 a)} \\[2ex]
\dot{\tilde{\theta}}(t) = \overline{\varphi}(t) \, \dfrac{\varepsilon(t)}{r(t)} & \text{(B.4 b)} \\[2ex]
\dot{r}(t) = - \lambda r(t) + |\overline{\varphi}(t)|^2 + \alpha(t); \quad \lambda > 0; & \text{(B.4 c)} \\[1ex]
\quad \begin{matrix} \lambda r_{min} \leq \alpha(t) \leq \overline{\alpha}, \; r(t) \leq r_{min}, \\ 0 \leq \alpha(t) \leq \overline{\alpha}, \; r(t) > r_{min}, \end{matrix} \quad r(0) \geq r_{min} > 0 & \\[2ex]
\varepsilon(t) = e_f(t) - \hat{e}_f(t) & \text{(B.4 d)} \\[2ex]
\hat{e}_f(t) = \hat{b}_0(t) \left[\dfrac{\overline{u}(t)}{P_1} + \hat{\theta}^T(t) \, \overline{\varphi}(t)\right]. & \text{(B.4 e)}
\end{cases}$$

- control law:

$$\frac{\overline{u}(t)}{P_1} = - \left[\frac{P_1(0)}{P_1} \hat{\theta}^T(t)\right] \overline{\varphi}(t). \tag{B.4 f}$$

Assume that assumptions A.1 - A.4 are fulfilled. Further assume that the parameter estimates are uniformly bounded. Then the closed loop is L^{∞}-stable, i.e. if $v(t)$ and $u^M(t)$ are uniformly bounded, then $u(t)$ and $y(t)$ are also uniformly bounded.

Proof

A single realization will be considered throughout the proof. The boundedness of $|\overline{\varphi}(t)|$ will be proved by contradiction. Thus, assume that

$$\sup_{t \geq 0} |\overline{\varphi}(t)| > NM$$

for N and M arbitrarily large. This assumption will be contradicted for some N and M. Assuming the unboundedness, t_{NM} and t_M are well-defined if $N > 1$ and $M > |\overline{\varphi}(0)|$:

$$t_{NM} = \min \{t |\ |\overline{\varphi}(t)| = NM \}$$

$$t_M = \max \{t |\ t < t_{NM};\ |\overline{\varphi}(t)| = M;$$
$$|\overline{\varphi}(s)| < M \ \forall \ s \in (\max(0, t-c_M \ln N), t) \}.$$

Here the continuity of $|\overline{\varphi}(t)|$ is used. The constant c_M will be defined below. A typical realization of $|\overline{\varphi}(t)|$ in the time interval $[t_M, t_{NM}]$ is shown in Fig. B.1.

The contradiction will follow from thorough analysis of the algorithm in the interval $[t_M, t_{NM}]$. An outline of the proof is as follows. In Step 1 an increasing sequence $\{|\overline{\varphi}(\tau_i)|\}_{i=1}^{N_\tau}$ in the interval $[t_M, t_{NM}]$ is defined and a lower bound on N_τ is given. Step 2 derives an upper bound on $\tau_{N_\tau} - \tau_1$. Finally, Step 3 derives an upper bound on N_τ which is in disagreement with the result in Step 1 and the boundedness of $|\overline{\varphi}(t)|$ is thereby proved. The boundedness of $u(t)$ and $y(t)$ is then easily concluded.

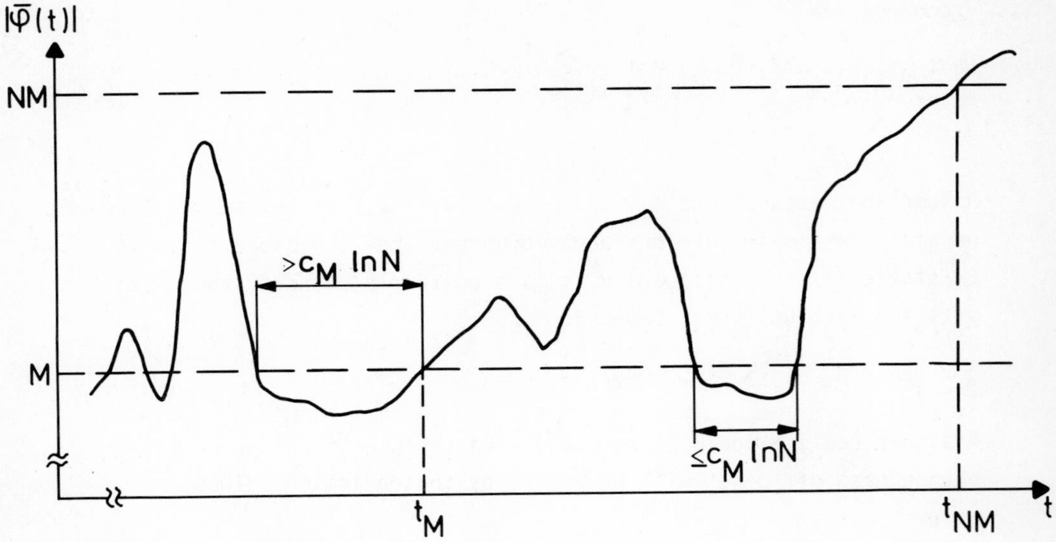

Figure B.1. The behaviour of $|\overline{\varphi}(t)|$ in the interval $[t_M, t_{NM}]$.

Before proceeding to the main part of the proof, some results are given in the form of separate lemmas. Proofs of these lemmas are found at the end of the appendix.

LEMMA B.1

Under the conditions of the theorem, there exist positive constants a and K and an asymptotically stable matrix F such that, for every $t \geq s+1$,

$$|\overline{\varphi}(t)| \leq K\left[\|e^{F(t-s)}\| \ |\overline{\varphi}(s)| + (t-s)\left(1 + \sup_{s\leq\tau\leq t} \int_0^\tau e^{-a(\tau-\sigma)} |e_f(\sigma)|d\sigma\right)\right]. \tag{B.5}$$

LEMMA B.2

Under the conditions of the theorem, there exist positive constants K_1 and K_2 such that

$$|\overline{\varphi}(t)| \leq e^{K_1(t-s)}(|\overline{\varphi}(s)| + K_2) \quad \forall\, t \geq s. \tag{B.6}$$

LEMMA B.3

Under the conditions of the theorem, there exists a positive constant K_3 such that

$$\frac{|\bar{\varphi}(t)|^2}{r(t)} \leqslant K_3 \quad \forall\, t. \tag{B.7}$$

LEMMA B.4

Under the conditions of the theorem, there exist positive constants K_4, K_5, and c such that for arbitrary T,

$$|\hat{e}_f(t)| \leqslant K_4\, e^{-cT} |\bar{\varphi}(t)| + K_5\, e^{K_1 T} \int_{t-T}^{t} |\varepsilon(s)|\, ds \quad \forall\, t \geqslant T \tag{B.8}$$

where K_1 is as in Lemma B.2.

Before returning to the proof of the theorem, an important observation will be made. First choose

$$c_M = \max\left(\frac{2}{\lambda}, \frac{1}{a}\right) \tag{B.9}$$

with a from Lemma B.1. Let $[s_1, s_2]$ be any interval between t_M and t_{NM} such that

$$\begin{cases} |\bar{\varphi}(s_2)| = M \\ |\bar{\varphi}(s)| < M \quad \forall\, s_1 < s < s_2. \end{cases}$$

If $\min\limits_{s_1 \leqslant s \leqslant s_2} |\bar{\varphi}(s)|$ is attained for $s = s_0$, Lemma B.2 and the definition of t_M give

$$M = |\bar{\varphi}(s_2)| \leqslant e^{K_1(s_2 - s_0)} (|\bar{\varphi}(s_0)| + K_2) \leqslant e^{K_1 c_M \ln N} (|\bar{\varphi}(s_0)| + K_2)$$

which implies

$$|\bar{\varphi}(s_0)| \geqslant \frac{M}{N^{K_1 c_M}} - K_2.$$

Since the interval $[s_1, s_2]$ is arbitrary, we thus have

$$\min_{t_M \leq s \leq t_{NM}} |\bar{\varphi}(s)| \geq \frac{M}{N^{K_1 c_M}} - K_2. \tag{B.10}$$

Step 1. Characterization of the sequence $\{\bar{\varphi}(\tau_i)\}$

The sequence $\{\tau_i\}_{i=1}^{N_\tau}$ is defined recursively from

$$\begin{cases} \tau_1 = t_M \\ \tau_{i+1} = \inf \{ t \mid \tau_i + n_\tau \leq t < t_{NM}, \ |\bar{\varphi}(t)| \geq \sup_{t_M \leq s \leq t} |\bar{\varphi}(s)| \}, \end{cases}$$

where n_τ will be defined below. The sequence $\{\tau_i\}$ for the realization in Fig. B.1 is shown in Fig. B.2.

Let $N_F(x)$ be the smallest number that satisfies

$$\| K e^{Ft} \| \leq \frac{1}{x} \quad \forall \ t \geq N_F(x) \qquad (x > 0) \tag{B.11}$$

where K and F are from Lemma B.1. The definition is meaningful because

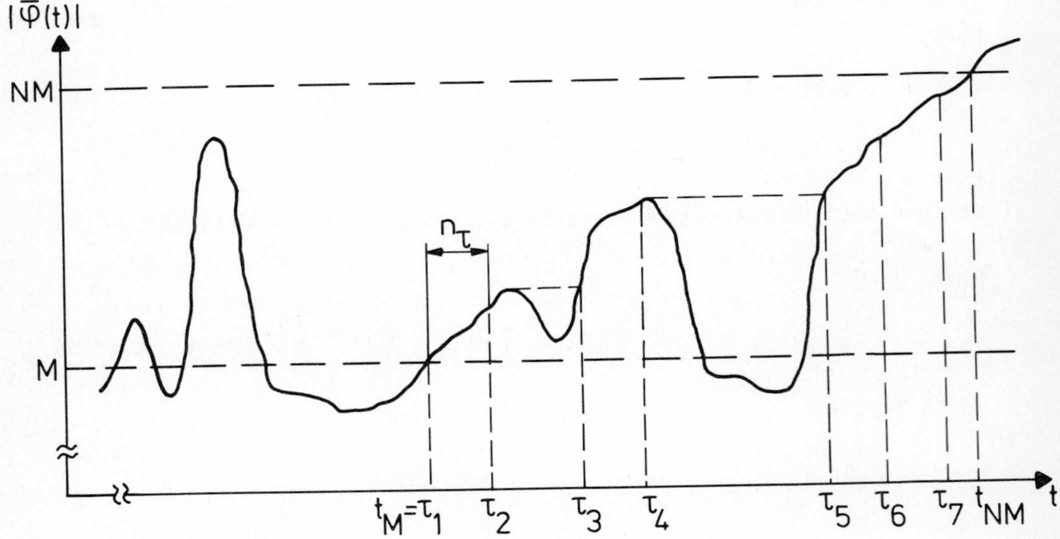

Figure B.2. The definition of $\{\tau_i\}$.

F has its eigenvalues in the open left half plane. Also note that from (B.2), (B.4 f), and the boundedness of the estimates and the noise it follows that for some K_e, K_v

$$|e_f(t)| \leq K_e \, |\overline{\varphi}(t)| + K_v \quad \forall\, t. \tag{B.12}$$

Now choose n_τ in the definition of $\{\tau_i\}$ to be a number which fulfills the following conditions:

$$\begin{aligned}
&\text{(i)} \quad n_\tau \geq 1 \\
&\text{(ii)} \quad n_\tau \geq N_F(5) \\
&\text{(iii)} \quad n_\tau \, e^{-\frac{an_\tau}{2}} \leq \frac{a}{10K(K_e+1)} \\
&\text{(iv)} \quad n_\tau \, e^{-\frac{cn_\tau}{2}} \leq \frac{a}{5KK_4} .
\end{aligned} \tag{B.13}$$

Here a and K are from Lemma B.1, K_e as in (B.12), and c and K_4 from Lemma B.4.

Let M satisfy the condition

$$M \geq K_2$$

with K_2 as in Lemma B.2. It should be noted that N and M can be chosen arbitrarily. A number of conditions of the type above will appear in the proof. They are however easy to fulfill by choosing N and M appropriately. It is, however, important that the constants appearing in the conditions do not depend on the choice of interval $[t_M, t_{NM}]$, i.e. on N and M themselves. This fact will not be commented upon in the sequel.

If M is chosen to fulfill the condition above, Lemma B.2 gives rise to an inequality in the following way. Separate between two cases:

(i) $\tau_{i+1} = \tau_i + n_\tau$; then

$$|\overline{\varphi}(\tau_{i+1})| \leq 2e^{K_1 n_\tau} \, |\overline{\varphi}(\tau_i)|.$$

(ii) $\tau_{i+1} > \tau_i + n_\tau$; the definition of $\{\tau_i\}$ then implies

$$|\overline{\varphi}(\tau_i + n_\tau)| < \sup_{\tau_i \leq s \leq \tau_i + n_\tau} |\overline{\varphi}(s)|$$

and the continuity gives

$$|\overline{\varphi}(\tau_{i+1})| = \sup_{\tau_i \leq s \leq \tau_i + n_\tau} |\overline{\varphi}(s)| \leq 2e^{K_1 n_\tau} |\overline{\varphi}(\tau_i)|.$$

The same inequality thus holds in both cases. Using this together with the fact that

$$t_{NM} - \tau_{N_\tau} < n_\tau,$$

which follows from the definition of $\{\tau_i\}$ and the continuity, the following is obtained:

$$NM = |\overline{\varphi}(t_{NM})| \leq 2e^{K_1 n_\tau} |\overline{\varphi}(\tau_{N_\tau})| \leq \ldots \leq 2^{N_\tau} e^{K_1 n_\tau N_\tau} |\varphi(\tau_1)| =$$
$$= 2^{N_\tau} e^{K_1 n_\tau N_\tau} M$$

which implies

$$N_\tau \geq \frac{\ln N}{\ln 2 + K_1 n_\tau} . \qquad \text{(B.14)}$$

This is the lower bound on N_τ sought for in Step 1.

Step 2. Derivation of an upper bound on $\tau_{N_\tau} - \tau_1$

Define intervals

$$I_i = [\tau_{i-1}, \tau_{i+1}], \quad i = 2, 4, \ldots, 2N_I$$

where the number of intervals N_I satisfies

$$N_I = \begin{cases} \frac{1}{2}(N_\tau - 1), & N_\tau \text{ odd} \\ \frac{1}{2}(N_\tau - 2), & N_\tau \text{ even.} \end{cases} \qquad \text{(B.15)}$$

Consider an interval I_i and define the sequence $\{T_j^i\}_{j=0}^{N_T^i}$ inside the interval through

$$\begin{cases} T_0^i = \tau_{i-1} \\ T_j^i = \min\{t \mid t \geq T_{j-1}^i + n_T,\ |\overline{\varphi}(t)| \geq M\},\ j = 1,\ldots,N_T^i \end{cases} \tag{B.16}$$

where N_T^i satisfies

$$\tau_{i+1} - n_T \leq T_{N_T^i}^i \leq \tau_{i+1}. \tag{B.17}$$

The left inequality follows because $|\overline{\varphi}(\tau_{i+1})| \geq M$. The constant n_T is defined as

$$n_T = K_T \ln N, \tag{B.18}$$

where

$$K_T = \max\left(\frac{2}{-r(F)}, \frac{2}{c\rho}\right). \tag{B.19}$$

Here $r(F)$ is the largest real part of any eigenvalue of F and ρ is defined as

$$\rho = \frac{a}{a+c}. \tag{B.20}$$

Let ΔT be the maximal distance between any T_j^i and T_{j+1}^i. It follows from the definition of t_M (cf. Fig. B.1) and (B.16) that

$$\Delta T \leq n_T + c_M \ln N = (K_T + c_M) \ln N \triangleq K_\Delta \ln N, \tag{B.21}$$

where K_Δ is independent of N.

Define intervals

$$J_j^i = [T_{j-1}^i, T_{j+1}^i], \quad j = 1, 3, \ldots, 2N_J^i - 1,$$

where the number of intervals N_J^i satisfies

$$N_J^i = \begin{cases} \frac{1}{2}(N_T^i - 1), & N_T^i \text{ odd}, \\ \frac{1}{2} N_T^i, & N_T^i \text{ even}. \end{cases} \tag{B.22}$$

The behaviour of the algorithm in an interval J_j^i will now be examined.

Distinguish between two cases.

The case $N_T^i \geq 2$

From (B.22) it is seen that there is at least one interval J_j^i in the interval I_i. Suppose that

$$\int_{T_{j-1}^i}^{T_{j+1}^i} |\varepsilon(s)|\, ds < \frac{M}{4K\,(1+\frac{K_5}{a})\,\Delta T\, e^{K_1 \rho n_T}} . \qquad (B.23)$$

This will lead to a contradiction. To see this, we will first show that $n_T \geq N_F(4N)$. The matrix F used when defining $N_F(x)$, (B.11), has its eigenvalues in the open left half plane. This implies the existence of a constant K_F such that, for some t_F,

$$\| e^{Ft} \| \leq K_F\, e^{t \cdot r(F)} \qquad \forall\, t \geq t_F,$$

where r(F) is defined in connection with (B.19). Clearly $N_F(4N) \to \infty$, $N \to \infty$. Then it follows by continuity of $\| e^{Ft} \|$ from (B.11) that

$$\frac{1}{4N} = K\, \| e^{FN_F(4N)} \| \leq KK_F\, e^{N_F(4N) \cdot r(F)}$$

for N sufficiently large and so

$$N_F(4N) \leq \frac{\ln N + \ln 4KK_F}{-r(F)} \leq \frac{2}{-r(F)} \ln N \leq n_T .$$

It is thus possible to use Lemma B.1 and the definitions of $N_F(4N)$ and ΔT to obtain

$$|\overline{\varphi}(T_{j+1}^i)| \leq \frac{|\overline{\varphi}(T_j^i)|}{4N} + K\Delta T \left(1 + \sup_{T_j^i \leq \tau \leq T_{j+1}^i} \int_0^\tau e^{-a(\tau-\sigma)} |e_f(\sigma)|\, d\sigma \right).$$

Suppose the sup is attained for $\tau = t$. Then

$$|\overline{\varphi}(T_{j+1}^i)| \leq \frac{|\overline{\varphi}(T_j^i)|}{4N} + K\Delta T\, (1 + \int_0^t e^{-a(t-\sigma)} |e_f(\sigma)|\, d\sigma) \leq$$

$$\leq \frac{NM}{4N} + K\Delta T + K\Delta T\, e^{-a(t-T^i_{j-1}-T)} \int_0^{T^i_{j-1}+T} e^{-a(T^i_{j-1}+T-\sigma)} |e_f(\sigma)|\, d\sigma +$$

$$+ K\Delta T \int_{T^i_{j-1}+T}^{t} e^{-a(t-\sigma)} |e_f(\sigma)|\, d\sigma \;\hat{=}\; \frac{M}{4} + K\Delta T + R_1 + R_2, \qquad \text{(B.24)}$$

where $0 < T < n_T$ will be chosen later. The two terms R_1 and R_2 will be estimated separately. From (B.12) and the definition of $\{T^i_j\}$ it follows that

$$R_1 \leq K\Delta T\, e^{-a(n_T-T)} \frac{1}{a} \sup_{\sigma \leq T^i_j} |e_f(\sigma)| \leq$$

$$\leq K\Delta T\, e^{-a(n_T-T)} \frac{1}{a} \sup_{\sigma \leq T^i_j} (K_e|\overline{\varphi}(\sigma)| + K_v) \leq \frac{K}{a}(K_e+1)\, \Delta T\, e^{-a(n_T-T)} NM,$$

if N and M are chosen such that $K_v \leq NM$. The term R_2 is estimated using (B.4 d) and Lemma B.4:

$$R_2 \leq K\Delta T \int_{T^i_{j-1}+T}^{t} \Big(|\varepsilon(\sigma)| + e^{-a(t-\sigma)} |\hat{e}_f(\sigma)| \Big) d\sigma \leq K\Delta T \int_{T^i_{j-1}}^{T^i_{j+1}} |\varepsilon(\sigma)|\, d\sigma +$$

$$+ K\Delta T \Big[\int_{T^i_{j-1}+T}^{t} e^{-a(t-\sigma)} \Big(K_4 e^{-cT} |\overline{\varphi}(\sigma)| + K_5 e^{K_1 T} \int_{\sigma-T}^{\sigma} |\varepsilon(s)|\, ds \Big) d\sigma \Big] \leq$$

$$\leq K\Delta T \Big(1 + \frac{K_5}{a} e^{K_1 T} \Big) \int_{T^i_{j-1}}^{T^i_{j+1}} |\varepsilon(s)|\, ds + \frac{K}{a} K_4 \Delta T\, e^{-cT} NM.$$

Now choose $T = \rho \cdot n_T$ and use (B.20) to obtain for large N

$$R_1 + R_2 \leq \frac{K\Delta T}{a} \Big((K_e+1)\, e^{-a(1-\rho)n_T} + K_4\, e^{-c\rho n_T} \Big) NM +$$

$$+ K\Delta T \Big(1 + \frac{K_5}{a} e^{K_1 \rho n_T} \Big) \int_{T^i_{j-1}}^{T^i_{j+1}} |\varepsilon(s)|\, ds \leq$$

$$\leq \frac{K\Delta T}{a} (K_e+K_4+1)\, e^{-c\rho n_T}\, NM + K\Delta T \left(1 + \frac{K_5}{a}\right) e^{K_1 \rho n_T} \int_{T_{j-1}^i}^{T_{j+1}^i} |\varepsilon(s)|\, ds <$$

$$< \frac{K}{a} (K_e+K_4+1)\, K_\Delta \ln N\, e^{-c\rho K_T \ln N}\, NM + \frac{M}{4} \leq \frac{M}{2}, \tag{B.25}$$

where (B.18), (B.21), and the assumption (B.23) have been used in the second last step and the definition of K_T, (B.19), was used in the last step. If (B.25) is inserted into (B.24), the result is

$$|\bar{\varphi}(T_{j+1}^i)| < M$$

if

$$K\Delta T \leq \frac{M}{4}.$$

This is trivially satisfied for large N by the choice

$$M = N^p \triangleq N^{K_1(c_M + \rho K_T) + 4} \tag{B.26}$$

With this choice of M, we have arrived at a contradiction and the conclusion is that

$$\int_{T_{j-1}^i}^{T_{j+1}^i} |\varepsilon(s)|\, ds \geq \frac{M}{4K\left(1 + \frac{K_5}{a}\right) \Delta T\, e^{K_1 \rho n_T}}. \tag{B.27}$$

The inequality holds for every interval J_j^i. Define

$$V(t) = \tilde{b}_0^2(t) + b_0\, \tilde{\theta}^T(t)\, \tilde{\theta}(t). \tag{B.28}$$

Lemma 5.1 gives

$$V(T_{j+1}^i) - V(T_{j-1}^i) \leq -\int_{T_{j-1}^i}^{T_{j+1}^i} \frac{\varepsilon^2(s)}{r(s)}\, ds + \int_{T_{j-1}^i}^{T_{j+1}^i} \left(\frac{AR}{P}\, \bar{v}(s)\right)^2 \frac{ds}{r(s)} \leq$$

$$\leq -\int_{T_{j-1}^i}^{T_{j+1}^i} \frac{\varepsilon^2(s)}{r(s)}\, ds + \int_{T_{j-1}^i}^{T_{j+1}^i} \frac{K_v^2}{r(s)}\, ds,$$

where K_v is the bound on the noise introduced in (B.12). Note that, for $T^i_{j-1} \leqslant s \leqslant T^i_{j+1}$,

$$r(s) = e^{-\lambda s} r(0) + \int_0^s e^{-\lambda(s-\sigma)}(|\overline{\varphi}(\sigma)|^2 + \alpha(\sigma))\, d\sigma \leqslant$$

$$\leqslant r(0) + \frac{\overline{\alpha}}{\lambda} + \frac{(NM)^2}{\lambda} \leqslant \frac{2}{\lambda}(NM)^2$$

if N and M are chosen sufficiently large. Furthermore, it follows from Lemma B.3, (B.10), and (B.26) that, for large N,

$$r(s) \geqslant \frac{1}{K_3} |\overline{\varphi}(s)|^2 \geqslant \frac{1}{K_3}\left(\frac{M}{N^{K_1 c_M}} - K_2\right)^2 \geqslant \frac{1}{2K_3} N^{2(p-K_1 c_M)}. \qquad (B.29)$$

Apply these two inequalities above to obtain

$$V(T^i_{j+1}) - V(T^i_{j-1}) \leqslant -\frac{\lambda}{2(NM)^2} \int_{T^i_{j-1}}^{T^i_{j+1}} \varepsilon^2(s)\, ds + \frac{4\Delta T\, K_v^2\, K_3}{N^{2(p-K_1 c_M)}}.$$

Now, use Schwarz' inequality to obtain for N sufficiently large:

$$V(T^i_{j+1}) - V(T^i_{j-1}) \leqslant -\frac{\lambda}{2(NM)^2} \cdot \frac{1}{(T^i_{j+1} - T^i_{j-1})}\left[\int_{T^i_{j-1}}^{T^i_{j+1}} |\varepsilon(s)|\, ds\right]^2 +$$

$$+ \frac{4\Delta T\, K_v^2\, K_3}{N^{2(p-K_1 c_M)}} \leqslant -\frac{\lambda}{4\Delta T(NM)^2}\left[\int_{T^i_{j-1}}^{T^i_{j+1}} |\varepsilon(s)|\, ds\right]^2 + \frac{4\Delta T\, K_v^2\, K_3}{N^{2(p-K_1 c_M)}} \leqslant$$

$$\leqslant -\frac{\lambda}{4\Delta T\, N^2\left[4K\left(1 + \frac{K_5}{a}\right)\Delta T\, e^{K_1 \rho n_T}\right]^2} + \frac{4\Delta T\, K_v^2\, K_3}{N^{2(p-K_1 c_M)}} \triangleq$$

$$\triangleq -\frac{c_1}{N^2\, \Delta T^3\, e^{2K_1 \rho n_T}} + \frac{c_2\, \Delta T}{N^{2(p-K_1 c_M)}}, \qquad (B.30)$$

where c_1 and c_2 are independent of N.

It follows from (B.18) and (B.21) that

$$\Delta T^3 \, e^{2K_1 \rho n_T} \leqslant K_\Delta^3 \, N^3 \, N^{2K_1 \rho K_T}.$$

Inserting this inequality into (B.30) and also using (B.26) gives

$$V(T^i_{j+1}) - V(T^i_{j-1}) \leqslant - \frac{c_1}{N^2 \, K_\Delta^3 \, N^3 \, N^{2K_1 \rho K_T}} + \frac{c_2 \, K_\Delta \, N}{N^{2(K_1 \rho K_T + 4)}} =$$

$$= - \frac{1}{N^{2K_1 \rho K_T + 5}} \left[\frac{c_1}{K_\Delta^3} - c_2 \, K_\Delta \frac{N^{2(K_1 \rho K_T + 3)}}{N^{2(K_1 \rho K_T + 4)}} \right] \leqslant$$

$$\leqslant - \frac{c_0}{N^{2K_1 \rho K_T + 5}} \triangleq - \frac{c_0}{N^{p_0}}, \qquad \text{N sufficiently large,}$$

where c_0 is a constant, independent of N.

This inequality holds for every interval J^i_j, i.e. N^i_J times, whence

$$V\left(T^i_{2N^i_J}\right) - V(T^i_0) \leqslant - c_0 \frac{N^i_J}{N^{p_0}}.$$

But V is positive and also from the assumptions bounded, by $\tilde{K}_V$ say, so that

$$N^i_J \leqslant \frac{\tilde{K}_V}{c_0} \cdot N^{p_0}. \qquad \text{(B.31)}$$

The case $N^i_T < 2$

The inequality (B.31) is trivially satisfied also in this case, because $N^i_T < 2$ implies $N^i_J = 0$.

The conclusion is thus that (B.31) holds in every interval I_i provided N is chosen large enough. From (B.17) and (B.22) it follows that

$$\tau_{i+1} - T^i_{2N^i_J} = \left(\tau_{i+1} - T^i_{N^i_T}\right) + \left(T^i_{N^i_T} - T^i_{2N^i_J}\right) \leqslant n_T + \Delta T \leqslant 2\Delta T$$

which together with (B.31) gives

$$\tau_{i+1} - \tau_{i-1} = \left(\tau_{i+1} - T^i_{2N^i_J}\right) + \left(T^i_{2N^i_J} - T^i_0\right) \leqslant 2\Delta T + 2N^i_J \Delta T \leqslant$$

$$\leqslant 2\Delta T \left(1 + \frac{\tilde{K}_v}{c_0} \cdot N^{p_0}\right) \leqslant \frac{4\tilde{K}_v}{c_0} \Delta T \cdot N^{p_0}.$$

Summing for $i = 2, 4, \ldots, 2N_I$ gives

$$\tau_{2N_I+1} - \tau_1 \leqslant \frac{4\tilde{K}_v}{c_0} \Delta T \cdot N^{p_0} \cdot N_I \tag{B.32}$$

which concludes Step 2 of the proof.

<u>Step 3. Derivation of an upper bound on N_τ and the contradiction</u>

Consider an interval I_i defined in Step 2. Suppose that

$$\int_{\tau_{i+1}-2n_\tau}^{\tau_{i+1}} |\varepsilon(s)|\, ds < \frac{|\overline{\varphi}(\tau_{i+1})|}{5Kn_\tau\left(1 + \frac{K_5}{a} e^{K_1 n_\tau/2}\right)} . \tag{B.33}$$

This assumption will lead to a contradiction in much the same way as in Step 2. Analogously with (B.24) we have

$$|\overline{\varphi}(\tau_{i+1})| \leqslant \frac{|\overline{\varphi}(\tau_{i+1} - n_\tau)|}{5} + Kn_\tau + R_1 + R_2,$$

where

$$R_1 = Kn_\tau\, e^{-a(t-\tau_{i+1}+\frac{3}{2}n_\tau)} \int_0^{\tau_{i+1}-\frac{3}{2}n_\tau} e^{-a(\tau_{i+1}-\frac{3}{2}n_\tau-\sigma)} |e_f(\sigma)|\, d\sigma$$

$$R_2 = Kn_\tau \int_{\tau_{i+1}-\frac{3}{2}n_\tau}^{t} e^{-a(t-\sigma)} |e_f(\sigma)|\, d\sigma$$

and t is in the interval $[\tau_{i+1} - n_\tau, \tau_{i+1}]$. The properties (B.13 i, ii) of n_τ has been used. The term R_1 can be bounded from above using (B.9) and (B.12) if $K_v \leqslant M = N^p$, which is true for large enough N:

$$R_1 \leqslant Kn_\tau e^{-\frac{an_\tau}{2}} \left[e^{-a[\tau_{i+1} - \frac{3}{2}n_\tau - (t_M - c_M \ln N)]} \int_0^{t_M - c_M \ln N} e^{-a(t_M - c_M \ln N - \sigma)} |e_f(\sigma)| d\sigma \right.$$

$$\left. + \int_{t_M - c_M \ln N}^{\tau_{i+1} - \frac{3}{2}n_\tau} e^{-a(\tau_{i+1} - \frac{3}{2}n_\tau - \sigma)} |e_f(\sigma)| \, d\sigma \right] \leqslant$$

$$\leqslant Kn_\tau e^{-\frac{an_\tau}{2}} (K_e + 1) \left[e^{-a\, c_M \ln N} \cdot \frac{NM}{a} + \frac{|\overline{\varphi}(\tau_{i+1})|}{a} \right] \leqslant$$

$$\leqslant Kn_\tau e^{-\frac{an_\tau}{2}} (K_e + 1) \left[\frac{M}{a} + \frac{|\overline{\varphi}(\tau_{i+1})|}{a} \right] \leqslant$$

$$\leqslant Kn_\tau e^{-\frac{an_\tau}{2}} (K_e + 1) \frac{2}{a} |\overline{\varphi}(\tau_{i+1})| \leqslant \frac{|\overline{\varphi}(\tau_{i+1})|}{5},$$

where (B.13 iii) has been used in the last step. The term R_2 is estimated exactly as in Step 2:

$$R_2 \leqslant Kn_\tau \left(1 + \frac{K_5}{a} e^{K_1 n_\tau / 2} \right) \int_{\tau_{i+1} - 2n_\tau}^{\tau_{i+1}} |\varepsilon(s)| \, ds + \frac{K}{a} K_4 n_\tau e^{-\frac{cn_\tau}{2}} |\overline{\varphi}(\tau_{i+1})| <$$

$$< \frac{|\overline{\varphi}(\tau_{i+1})|}{5} + \frac{|\overline{\varphi}(\tau_{i+1})|}{5},$$

where (B.13 iv) and the assumption (B.33) have been used in the last step. Using the estimates of R_1 and R_2, we thus have

$$|\overline{\varphi}(\tau_{i+1})| < \frac{|\overline{\varphi}(\tau_{i+1} - n_\tau)|}{5} + Kn_\tau + \frac{3}{5} |\overline{\varphi}(\tau_{i+1})| \leqslant |\overline{\varphi}(\tau_{i+1})|$$

if

$$Kn_\tau \leqslant \frac{M}{5} = \frac{N^p}{5},$$

which of course is satisfied for large N. We have thus arrived at a contradiction and the conclusion is that

$$\int_{\tau_{i+1}-2n_\tau}^{\tau_{i+1}} |\varepsilon(s)|\, ds \geq \frac{|\bar{\varphi}(\tau_{i+1})|}{5Kn_\tau\left(1+\frac{K_5}{a}e^{K_1 n_\tau/2}\right)}. \tag{B.34}$$

The inequality holds for every interval I_i. From (B.9) it follows that, for $\tau_{i-1} \leq s \leq \tau_{i+1}$,

$$r(s) = e^{-\lambda s} r(0) + \int_0^s e^{-\lambda(s-\sigma)}[\,|\bar{\varphi}(\sigma)|^2 + \alpha(\sigma)]\, d\sigma \leq$$

$$\leq r(0) + \frac{\bar{\alpha}}{\lambda} + \int_0^s e^{-\lambda(s-\sigma)} |\bar{\varphi}(\sigma)|^2\, d\sigma =$$

$$= r(0) + \frac{\bar{\alpha}}{\lambda} + e^{-\lambda(s-t_M+c_M \ln N)} \int_0^{t_M-c_M \ln N} e^{-\lambda(t_M-c_M \ln N-\sigma)} |\bar{\varphi}(\sigma)|^2\, d\sigma +$$

$$+ \int_{t_M-c_M \ln N}^{s} e^{-\lambda(s-\sigma)} |\bar{\varphi}(\sigma)|^2\, d\sigma \leq$$

$$\leq r(0) + \frac{\bar{\alpha}}{\lambda} + e^{-\lambda c_M \ln N} \cdot \frac{(NM)^2}{\lambda} + \frac{|\bar{\varphi}(\tau_{i+1})|^2}{\lambda} \leq$$

$$\leq r(0) + \frac{\bar{\alpha}}{\lambda} + \frac{1}{\lambda}\left(M^2 + |\bar{\varphi}(\tau_{i+1})|^2\right) \leq \frac{3}{\lambda} |\bar{\varphi}(\tau_{i+1})|^2$$

for N sufficiently large. Applying Lemma 5.1 in the same way as in Step 2 now gives a result analogous with (B.30) for large N:

$$V(\tau_{i+1}) - V(\tau_{i-1}) \leq -\int_{\tau_{i-1}}^{\tau_{i+1}} \frac{\varepsilon^2(s)}{r(s)}\, ds + \int_{\tau_{i-1}}^{\tau_{i+1}} \left(\frac{AR}{P}\,\bar{v}(s)\right) \frac{ds}{r(s)} \leq$$

$$\leq -\int_{\tau_{i+1}-2n_\tau}^{\tau_{i+1}} \frac{\varepsilon^2(s)}{r(s)}\, ds + \int_{\tau_{i-1}}^{\tau_{i+1}} \frac{K_v^2}{r(s)}\, ds \leq$$

$$\leq -\frac{\lambda}{3|\varphi(\tau_{i+1})|^2}\cdot\frac{1}{2n_\tau}\left[\int_{\tau_{i+1}-2n_\tau}^{\tau_{i+1}}|\varepsilon(s)|\,ds\right]^2+\frac{2K_v^2K_3(\tau_{i+1}-\tau_{i-1})}{N^{2(p-K_1c_M)}}\leq$$

$$\leq -\frac{1}{6n_\tau\left[5Kn_\tau\left(1+\frac{K_5}{a}e^{K_1n_\tau/2}\right)\right]^2}+\frac{2K_v^2K_3(\tau_{i+1}-\tau_{i-1})}{N^{2(p-K_1c_M)}}\triangleq$$

$$\triangleq -c_3+c_4\frac{\tau_{i+1}-\tau_{i-1}}{N^{2(p-K_1c_M)}},$$

where c_3 and c_4 are independent of N and (B.34) has been used in the second last step. Summing the inequality for $i = 2, 4, \dots, 2N_I$ gives

$$V(\tau_{2N_I+1})-V(\tau_1)\leq -c_3N_I+c_4\frac{\tau_{2N_I+1}-\tau_1}{N^{2(p-K_1c_M)}}\leq$$

$$\leq -c_3N_I+c_4\frac{4\tilde{K}_v}{c_0}\cdot\frac{\Delta T\cdot N^{p_0}\cdot N_I}{N^{2(p-K_1c_M)}} = -N_I\left(c_3-c_4\frac{4\tilde{K}_v\,\Delta T}{c_0N^3}\right),$$

where (B.32) and the definitions of p_0 and p have been used. But V is positive and bounded by $\tilde{K}_v$ as in Step 2, so that

$$-\tilde{K}_v\leq -N_I\left(c_3-c_4\frac{4\tilde{K}_v\,\Delta T}{c_0N^3}\right)$$

which by (B.15) and (B.21) implies

$$N_\tau\leq 2N_I+2\leq\frac{2\tilde{K}_v}{\left|c_3-c_4\frac{4\tilde{K}_v\Delta T}{c_0N^3}\right|}+2\leq\frac{2\tilde{K}_v}{c_3-c_{3/2}}+2=\frac{4\tilde{K}_v}{c_3}+2$$

for N sufficiently large. This result obviously violates the inequality (B.14) obtained in Step 1 for N large enough. The existence of the sequence $\{|\overline{\varphi}(\tau_i)|\}$ for N arbitrarily large is thus contradicted and the boundedness of $|\overline{\varphi}(t)|$ is proved.

It remains to conclude boundedness of u(t) and y(t) from the boundedness of $|\overline{\varphi}(t)|$. From (B.2) and (B.4 f) it is clear that $e_f(t) = \frac{Q}{P}[y(t)-y^M(t)]$

is bounded. But $y^M(t)$ is bounded and Q and P are asymptotically stable polynomials of the same degree, which implies that y(t) is bounded.

The boundedness of u(t) is possible to establish from (B.4 f), which can be written

$$P_2 \frac{\overline{u}(t)}{P} = - \left(\frac{P_1(0)}{P_1} \hat{\theta}^T(t)\right) \overline{\varphi}(t)$$

or, using the definition of P_2,

$$p^{m+n_T} \frac{\overline{u}(t)}{P} = - \left(p_{21} p^{m+n_T-1} \frac{\overline{u}(t)}{P} + \ldots + p_{2(m+n_T)} \frac{\overline{u}(t)}{P}\right) -$$

$$- \left(\frac{P_1(0)}{P_1} \hat{\theta}^T(t)\right) \overline{\varphi}(t). \qquad (B.35)$$

Here all terms in the first bracket are components of $\overline{\varphi}(t)$ and it follows that $p^{m+n_T} \frac{\overline{u}(t)}{P}$ is bounded. Differentiating (B.35) 1, 2, ..., n-m-1 times gives recursively boundedness of $p^{m+n_T+1} \frac{\overline{u}(t)}{P}, \ldots, p^{n+n_T-1} \frac{\overline{u}(t)}{P}$. Notice that $\frac{\hat{\theta}(t)}{P_1}$ is possible to differentiate because P_1 is of degree n-m-1 and also that the derivatives of $\overline{\varphi}(t)$ are bounded because of earlier steps in the recursion and boundedness of y(t) and $u^M(t)$, cf. (B.3). Finally boundedness of $p^{n+n_T} \frac{\overline{u}(t)}{P}$ follows by an additional differentiation of (B.35) but then the boundedness of $\dot{\hat{\theta}}(t)$, which follows from (B.4 b,c,d), is also used. As a result, the first $n+n_T$ derivatives of $\frac{\overline{u}(t)}{P} = \frac{Q}{TA^M P} u(t)$ have been shown to be bounded. But the pole excess of $Q/TA^M P$ is exactly $n+n_T$ and Q is asymptotically stable. Hence boundedness of u(t) follows readily. The theorem is thus proven. □

Proof of Lemma B.1

Assume for the moment that $m \geq 1$ and define

$$\psi^T(t) = \left(\frac{p^{m+n_T-1}}{P} u(t), \ldots, \frac{p^{n_T}}{P} u(t) \right),$$

which thus is formed from the m first components of $\varphi(t)$. Using (B.1) and the definitions of e(t) and $e_f(t)$ (see (5.3)), the following is obtained:

$$\dot{\bar{\psi}}(t) = \begin{pmatrix} \frac{p^{m+n_T}}{P} \bar{u}(t) \\ \vdots \\ \frac{p^{n_T+1}}{P} \bar{u}(t) \end{pmatrix} =$$

$$= \begin{pmatrix} \frac{1}{b_0} \cdot \frac{p^{n_T} A}{P} [\bar{y}(t)-\bar{v}(t)] - b_1 \frac{p^{m+n_T-1}}{P} \bar{u}(t) - \ldots - b_m \frac{p^{n_T}}{P} \bar{u}(t) \\ \frac{p^{m+n_T-1}}{P} \bar{u}(t) \\ \vdots \\ \frac{p^{n_T+1}}{P} \bar{u}(t) \end{pmatrix} =$$

$$= \begin{pmatrix} -b_1 & \ldots & -b_m \\ 1 & & \\ & \ddots & \\ & 1 & 0 \end{pmatrix} \bar{\psi}(t) + \begin{pmatrix} \frac{1}{b_0} \frac{p^{n_T} A}{P} \bar{e}(t) \\ 0 \\ \vdots \\ 0 \end{pmatrix} + \begin{pmatrix} \frac{1}{b_0} \frac{p^{n_T} A}{P} [\bar{y}^M(t)-\bar{v}(t)] \\ 0 \\ \vdots \\ 0 \end{pmatrix} =$$

$$\triangleq F\overline{\psi}(t) + \begin{bmatrix} \frac{1}{b_0}\frac{p^{n_T}A}{TA^M}e_f(t) \\ 0 \\ \vdots \\ 0 \end{bmatrix} + b(t),$$

where F is asymptotically stable since the plant is minimum phase. Integrating from s to t gives

$$\overline{\psi}(t) = e^{F(t-s)}\,\overline{\psi}(s) + \int_s^t e^{F(t-\sigma)} \left\{ \begin{bmatrix} \frac{1}{b_0}\frac{p^{n_T}A}{TA^M}e_f(\sigma) \\ 0 \\ \vdots \\ 0 \end{bmatrix} + b(\sigma) \right\} d\sigma. \tag{B.36}$$

The vector b(t) is obtained by filtering $u^M(t)$ and v(t) (which are bounded) through proper, asymptotically stable filters and is therefore bounded by a constant K_b say. Also note that since F has its eigenvalues in the open left half plane,

$$\sup_{t\geq 0} \| e^{Ft} \| = K_F < \infty .$$

Finally we have

$$\left| \frac{1}{b_0}\frac{p^{n_T}A}{TA^M} e_f(t) \right| \leq K_1 \left(1 + \int_0^t e^{-a(t-s)}\,|e_f(s)|\,ds\right) \quad \forall\, t, \tag{B.37}$$

where a > 0, because $p^{n_T}A/TA^M$ is a proper, asymptotically stable transfer operator. Using these facts in (B.36) gives

$$|\overline{\psi}(t)| \leq \|e^{F(t-s)}\| \cdot |\overline{\psi}(s)| + K_F \int_s^t \left[K_1\left(1 + \int_0^\sigma e^{-a(\sigma-\tau)}|e_f(\tau)|d\tau\right) + K_b\right] d\sigma \leq$$

$$\leq \| e^{F(t-s)} \| \cdot |\overline{\psi}(s)| + K_2(t-s)\left[1 + \sup_{s\leq\sigma\leq t} \int_0^\sigma e^{-a(\sigma-\tau)}|e_f(\tau)|d\tau\right], \tag{B.38}$$

where $K_2 = K_F(K_1 + K_b)$.

The definitions of $\varphi(t)$ and $\psi(t)$ give

$$\bar{\varphi}(t) = \begin{pmatrix} \frac{p^{m+n_T-1}}{P}\,\bar{u}(t) \\ \vdots \\ \frac{\bar{u}(t)}{P} \\ \frac{p^{n-1}}{P}\,\bar{y}(t) \\ \vdots \\ \frac{\bar{y}(t)}{P} \\ -\frac{TB^M}{P}\,\bar{u}^M(t) \end{pmatrix} = \begin{pmatrix} \bar{\psi}(t) \\ \frac{p^{n_T-1}}{P}\,\bar{u}(t) \\ \vdots \\ \frac{\bar{u}(t)}{P} \\ \frac{p^{n-1}}{P}\,\bar{y}(t) \\ \vdots \\ \frac{\bar{y}(t)}{P} \\ -\frac{TB^M}{P}\,\bar{u}^M(t) \end{pmatrix} \tag{B.39}$$

From (B.1) it follows that, for $0 \leq i \leq n_T - 1$,

$$b_m p^i\, u(t) = \frac{1}{b_0}\,[p^{n+i}\, y(t) + \ldots + a_n p^i\, y(t) - p^i A v(t)] -$$
$$- p^{m+i}\, u(t) - \ldots - b_{m-1}\, p^{i+1}\, u(t),$$

where $b_m \neq 0$ from assumption (A.4) and so, because $v(t)$ is bounded,

$$\left|\frac{p^i}{P}\,\bar{u}(t)\right| \leq K_3\left(1 + \left|\frac{p^i}{P}\,\bar{y}(t)\right| + \ldots + \left|\frac{p^{n+i}}{P}\,\bar{y}(t)\right| + \right.$$
$$\left. + \left|\frac{p^{i+1}}{P}\,\bar{u}(t)\right| + \ldots + \left|\frac{p^{m+i}}{P}\,\bar{u}(t)\right|\right).$$

If this inequality is used recursively for $i = k, \ldots, n_T-1$, the following is obtained:

$$\left|\frac{p^k}{P}\,\bar{u}(t)\right| \leq K_4\left(1 + \left|\frac{\bar{y}(t)}{P}\right| + \ldots + \left|\frac{p^{n+n_T-1}}{P}\,\bar{y}(t)\right| + \right.$$
$$\left. + \left|\frac{p^{n_T}}{P}\,\bar{u}(t)\right| + \ldots + \left|\frac{p^{m+n_T-1}}{P}\,\bar{u}(t)\right|\right), \quad k = 0, \ldots, n_T-1.$$

Using the definition of $\psi(t)$, this can be simplified into

$$\left|\frac{p^k}{P}\,\bar{u}(t)\right| \leq K_5\left(1 + \left|\frac{\bar{y}(t)}{P}\right| + \ldots + \left|\frac{p^{n+n_T-1}}{P}\,\bar{y}(t)\right| + |\bar{\psi}(t)|\right),$$
$$k = 0, \ldots, n_T-1.$$

If this is used together with (B.39), the following estimate of $|\overline{\varphi}(t)|$ is obtained:

$$|\overline{\varphi}(t)| \leq K_6\left(1+\left|\frac{\overline{y}(t)}{P}\right|+\ldots+\left|\frac{p^{n+n_T-1}}{P}\overline{y}(t)\right|+|\overline{\psi}(t)|+\left|\frac{TB^M}{P}\overline{u}^M(t)\right|\right). \tag{B.40}$$

Here $(TB^M/P)\overline{u}^M(t)$ is bounded because $u^M(t)$ is bounded. Also, for $i = 0, \ldots, n+n_T-1$,

$$\frac{p^i}{P}\overline{y}(t) = \frac{p^i}{P}[\overline{e}(t)+\overline{y}^M(t)] = \frac{p^i}{TA^M}e_f(t) + \frac{p^i}{P}\overline{y}^M(t),$$

where the first term can be estimated as in (B.37) and the second term is bounded. The inequality (B.40) can therefore be simplified into

$$|\overline{\varphi}(t)| \leq K_7\left(1+\int_0^t e^{-a(t-\sigma)}|e_f(\sigma)|\,d\sigma + |\overline{\psi}(t)|\right).$$

Invoking (B.38) gives for $t-s \geq 1$

$$|\overline{\varphi}(t)| \leq K_7\left[1+\int_0^t e^{-a(t-\sigma)}|e_f(\sigma)|\,d\sigma + \|e^{F(t-s)}\|\cdot|\overline{\psi}(s)|\right.$$

$$\left.+\,K_2(t-s)\left(1+\sup_{s\leq\sigma\leq t}\int_0^\sigma e^{-a(\sigma-\tau)}|e_f(\tau)|\,d\tau\right)\right] \leq$$

$$\leq K\left[\|e^{F(t-s)}\|\cdot|\overline{\psi}(s)|+(t-s)\left(1+\sup_{s\leq\sigma\leq t}\int_0^\sigma e^{-a(\sigma-\tau)}|e_f(\tau)|\,d\tau\right)\right] \leq$$

$$\leq K\left[\|e^{F(t-s)}\|\cdot|\overline{\varphi}(s)|+(t-s)\left(1+\sup_{s\leq\sigma\leq t}\int_0^\sigma e^{-a(\sigma-\tau)}|e_f(\tau)|\,d\tau\right)\right].$$

It remains to comment the case $m=0$ when $\psi(t)$ is undefined. Then it is easy to see that (B.40) is valid without the $|\overline{\psi}(t)|$-term and the assertion of the lemma is still true. □

Proof of Lemma B.2

It follows from the definition of $\varphi(t)$, (B.3), that

$$\dot{\overline{\varphi}}(t) = \left[\begin{array}{cccc|cccc|c} 0 & & & & & & & & \\ 1 & & & & & & & & \\ & \ddots & & & & & & & \\ & & 1 & 0 & & & & & \\ \hline & & & & 0 & & & & \\ & & & & 1 & & & & \\ & & & & & \ddots & & & \\ & & & & & & 1 & 0 & \\ \hline & & & & & & & & 0 \end{array}\right] \overline{\varphi}(t) + \left[\begin{array}{c} \frac{p^{m+n_T}}{P}\overline{u}(t) \\ 0 \\ \frac{p^n}{P}\overline{y}(t) \\ 0 \\ -\frac{TB^M}{P}\dot{\overline{u}}^M(t) \end{array}\right] \tag{B.41}$$

From (B.4 f) it follows that

$$\frac{p^{m+n_T}}{P}\overline{u}(t) = \frac{p^{m+n_T} - P_2}{P}\overline{u}(t) + \frac{\overline{u}(t)}{P_1} =$$

$$= -\frac{p_{21}p^{m+n_T-1} + \ldots + p_{2(m+n_T)}}{P}\overline{u}(t) - \left[\frac{P_1(0)}{P_1}\hat{\theta}^T(t)\right]\overline{\varphi}(t) =$$

$$= -[p_{21} \ldots p_{2(m+n_T)} \quad 0 \ldots 0]\,\overline{\varphi}(t) - \left[\frac{P_1(0)}{P_1}\hat{\theta}^T(t)\right]\overline{\varphi}(t). \tag{B.42}$$

It can be seen from (B.1) that

$$\frac{p^n}{P}\overline{y}(t) = -\frac{a_1 p^{n-1} + \ldots + a_n}{P}\overline{y}(t) + b_0\frac{p^m + \ldots + b_m}{P}\overline{u}(t) + \frac{A}{P}\overline{v}(t),$$

which, if $n_T \geq 1$, can be rewritten as

$$\frac{p^n}{P}\overline{y}(t) = [0 \ldots 0 \quad b_0 \quad b_0b_1 \ldots b_0b_m \quad -a_1 \ldots -a_n \quad 0]\,\overline{\varphi}(t) + \frac{A}{P}\overline{v}(t) \tag{B.43}$$

whereas if $n_T = 0$ (B.42) gives

$$\frac{p^n}{P}\overline{y}(t) = [b_0b_1 \ldots b_0b_m \quad -a_1 \ldots -a_n \quad 0]\,\overline{\varphi}(t) -$$

$$- b_0[p_{21} \ldots p_{2m} \quad 0 \ldots 0]\,\overline{\varphi}(t) - b_0\left[\frac{P_1(0)}{P_1}\hat{\theta}^T(t)\right]\overline{\varphi}(t) + \frac{A}{P}\overline{v}(t). \tag{B.44}$$

If (B.42) and (B.43) or (B.44) are inserted into (B.41), the following is obtained:

$$\dot{\bar{\varphi}}(t) = A(t)\,\bar{\varphi}(t) + \begin{pmatrix} 0 \\ \vdots \\ 0 \\ \dfrac{QA}{TA^M P}\, v(t) \\ 0 \\ \vdots \\ 0 \\ -\dfrac{QB^M}{PA^M}\, \dot{u}^M(t) \end{pmatrix}$$

Here A(t) is a matrix with bounded elements according to the assumptions. Furthermore, QA/TA^MP and pQB^M/PA^M are proper, asymptotically stable transfer operators and v(t) and $u^M(t)$ are assumed bounded. Hence,

$$\dot{\bar{\varphi}}(t) = A(t)\,\bar{\varphi}(t) + b(t)$$

with a bounded vector b(t). This differential equation has the solution

$$\bar{\varphi}(t) = \phi(t,s)\,\bar{\varphi}(s) + \int_s^t \phi(t,\sigma)\, b(\sigma)\, d\sigma, \quad t \geq s \qquad \text{(B.45)}$$

where the transition matrix $\phi(t,s)$ satisfies

$$\phi(t,s) = I + \int_s^t A(\sigma)\, \phi(\sigma,s)\, d\sigma.$$

Using the boundedness of A(t), we have

$$\|\phi(t,s)\| \leq 1 + \int_s^t \|A(\sigma)\| \cdot \|\phi(\sigma,s)\|\, d\sigma \leq 1 + K_1 \int_s^t \|\phi(\sigma,s)\|\, d\sigma.$$

If the Groenwall-Bellman lemma is applied to this inequality, the result is

$$\|\phi(t,s)\| \leq e^{K_1(t-s)}$$

and so, using (B.45),

$$|\overline{\varphi}(t)| \leqslant \|\phi(t,s)\| \cdot |\overline{\varphi}(s)| + \int_s^t \|\phi(t,\sigma)\| \cdot |b(\sigma)| \, d\sigma \leqslant$$

$$\leqslant e^{K_1(t-s)} |\overline{\varphi}(s)| + \int_s^t e^{K_1(t-\sigma)} K_2 \, d\sigma \leqslant e^{K_1(t-s)}\left(|\varphi(s)| + \frac{K_2}{K_1}\right).$$

Replacing K_2/K_1 by K_2, the lemma is proven. □

Proof of Lemma B.3

The result is immediate for $0 \leqslant t \leqslant 1$, so it suffices to consider the case $t \geqslant 1$. From (B.4 c),

$$r(t) = e^{-\lambda t} r(0) + \int_0^t e^{-\lambda(t-s)}[|\overline{\varphi}(s)|^2 + \alpha(s)] \, ds \geqslant$$

$$\geqslant \int_{t-1}^t e^{-\lambda(t-s)} |\overline{\varphi}(s)|^2 \, ds \geqslant e^{-\lambda} \inf_{t-1\leqslant s\leqslant t} |\overline{\varphi}(s)|^2 \triangleq e^{-\lambda} |\overline{\varphi}(s_0)|^2 \tag{B.46}$$

for some $t-1 \leqslant s_0 \leqslant t$. But from Lemma B.2,

$$|\overline{\varphi}(t)| \leqslant e^{K_1}[|\overline{\varphi}(s_0)| + K_2]$$

which implies that

$$|\overline{\varphi}(t)|^2 \leqslant 2e^{2K_1}[|\overline{\varphi}(s_0)|^2 + K_2^2]$$

and so, using (B.46),

$$\frac{|\overline{\varphi}(t)|^2}{r(t)} \leqslant 2e^{2K_1}\left(e^{\lambda} + \frac{K_2^2}{r(t)}\right).$$

But from (B.4 c) it follows that

$$\dot{r}(t) \geqslant -\lambda r(t) + \alpha(t) \geqslant -\lambda r_{min} + \lambda r_{min} = 0 \qquad \text{if} \quad r(t) \leqslant r_{min}$$

so that, because $r(0) \geqslant r_{min}$,

$$r(t) \geqslant r_{min} \qquad \forall\, t.$$

If this is inserted into the inequality above, the lemma is proven. □

Proof of Lemma B.4

It is seen from (B.4 e,f,b) that

$$\hat{e}_f(t) = \hat{b}_0(t)\left(\frac{\overline{u(t)}}{P_1} + \hat{\theta}^T(t)\,\overline{\varphi}(t)\right) = \hat{b}_0(t)\left(\hat{\theta}^T(t) - \frac{P_1(0)}{P_1}\,\hat{\theta}^T(t)\right)\overline{\varphi}(t) =$$

$$= \hat{b}_0(t)[G(p)\,\dot{\hat{\theta}}^T(t)]\,\overline{\varphi}(t) = \hat{b}_0(t)\left(G(p)\,\frac{\overline{\varphi}^T(t)\,\varepsilon(t)}{r(t)}\right)\overline{\varphi}(t),$$

where

$$G(p) = \frac{[P_1(p) - P_1(0)]\,/\,p}{P_1(p)}$$

is a strictly proper, asymptotically stable transfer operator and $\hat{b}_0(t)$ is bounded. Hence,

$$|\hat{e}_f(t)| \leqslant K|\overline{\varphi}(t)|\left(e^{-ct} + \int_0^t e^{-c(t-s)}\,\frac{|\overline{\varphi}(s)|\cdot|\varepsilon(s)|}{r(s)}\,ds\right)$$

for some positive K and c. Split the integral into two parts:

$$|\hat{e}_f(t)| \leqslant K\,|\overline{\varphi}(t)|\left(e^{-ct} + \int_0^{t-T} e^{-c(t-s)}\,\frac{|\overline{\varphi}(s)|\cdot|\varepsilon(s)|}{r(s)}\,ds\right) +$$

$$+ K\,|\overline{\varphi}(t)|\int_{t-T}^{t} e^{-c(t-s)}\,\frac{|\overline{\varphi}(s)|\cdot|\varepsilon(s)|}{r(s)}\,ds. \qquad (B.47)$$

The two terms in the r.h.s. will be estimated separately. First use the boundedness of the estimates and the noise to conclude from (B.2) and (B.4 d,e,f) that for some K_ε and K_v,

$$|\varepsilon(t)| \leqslant K_\varepsilon\,|\overline{\varphi}(t)| + K_v.$$

Hence,

$$K\,|\overline{\varphi}(t)|\left(e^{-ct} + \int_0^{t-T} e^{-c(t-s)}\,\frac{|\overline{\varphi}(s)|\cdot|\varepsilon(s)|}{r(s)}\,ds\right) \leqslant$$

$$\leqslant K\,|\overline{\varphi}(t)|\,e^{-cT}\left(1 + \int_0^{t-T} e^{-c(t-T-s)}\,\frac{|\overline{\varphi}(s)|\cdot|\varepsilon(s)|}{r(s)}\,ds\right) \leqslant$$

$$\leq K|\bar{\varphi}(t)|\, e^{-cT}\left(1+\frac{1}{c}\sup_{s\leq t-T}\frac{|\bar{\varphi}(s)|\ (K_{\varepsilon}|\bar{\varphi}(s)|+K_{v})}{r(s)}\right)\leq$$

$$\leq K|\bar{\varphi}(t)|\, e^{-cT}\left(1+\frac{1}{c}\sup_{s\leq t-T}\frac{(K_{\varepsilon}+K_{v})\ |\bar{\varphi}(s)|^{2}+K_{v}}{r(s)}\right)\leq$$

$$\leq K|\bar{\varphi}(t)|\, e^{-cT}\left(1+\frac{1}{c}\,[K_{3}(K_{\varepsilon}+K_{v})]+\frac{K_{v}}{r_{min}}\right)\triangleq$$

$$\triangleq K_{4}\, e^{-cT}\ |\bar{\varphi}(t)|, \tag{B.48}$$

where Lemma B.3 and the lower bound on $r(t)$ obtained in the proof of that lemma have been used in the second last step. The second term in (B.47) is estimated by the use of Lemma B.2:

$$K\ |\bar{\varphi}(t)|\int_{t-T}^{t} e^{-c(t-s)}\,\frac{|\bar{\varphi}(s)|\cdot|\varepsilon(s)|}{r(s)}\, ds\leq$$

$$\leq K e^{K_{1}T}\int_{t-T}^{t} e^{-c(t-s)}[|\bar{\varphi}(s)|+K_{2}]\ \frac{|\bar{\varphi}(s)|\cdot|\varepsilon(s)|}{r(s)}\, ds\leq$$

$$\leq K e^{K_{1}T}\int_{t-T}^{t} e^{-c(t-s)}\ \frac{(K_{2}+1)\ |\bar{\varphi}(s)|^{2}+K_{2}}{r(s)}\ |\varepsilon(s)|\ ds\leq$$

$$\leq K e^{K_{1}T}\left((K_{2}+1)K_{3}+\frac{K_{2}}{r_{min}}\right)\int_{t-T}^{t}|\varepsilon(s)|\ ds\triangleq$$

$$\triangleq K_{5}\ e^{K_{1}T}\int_{t-T}^{t}|\varepsilon(s)|\ ds, \tag{B.49}$$

where the second last step follows as above. Inserting (B.48) and (B.49) into (B.47) proves the assertion of the lemma. □